# INCONSPICUOUS PROVIDENCE

THE GOSPEL ACCORDING TO
THE OLD TESTAMENT

*A series of studies on the lives of Old Testament characters, written for laypeople and pastors, and designed to encourage Christ-centered reading, teaching, and preaching of the Old Testament*

IAIN M. DUGUID
*Series Editor*

*After God's Own Heart*, by Mark J. Boda
*Crying Out for Vindication*, by David R. Jackson
*Faith in the Face of Apostasy*, by Raymond B. Dillard
*From Bondage to Liberty*, by Anthony T. Selvaggio
*From Famine to Fullness*, by Dean R. Ulrich
*Hope in the Midst of a Hostile World*, by George M. Schwab
*Immanuel in Our Place*, by Tremper Longman III
*Inconspicuous Providence*, by Bryan R. Gregory
*Living in the Gap Between Promise and Reality*, by Iain M. Duguid
*Living in the Grip of Relentless Grace*, by Iain M. Duguid
*Living in the Light of Inextinguishable Hope*, by Iain M. Duguid and Matthew P. Harmon
*Longing for God in an Age of Discouragement*, by Bryan R. Gregory
*Love Divine and Unfailing*, by Michael P. V. Barrett
*Recovering Eden*, by Zack Eswine
*Right in Their Own Eyes*, by George M. Schwab
*Salvation Through Judgment and Mercy*, by Bryan D. Estelle

# INCONSPICUOUS PROVIDENCE

## THE GOSPEL ACCORDING TO ESTHER

BRYAN R. GREGORY

P.O. BOX 817 • PHILLIPSBURG • NEW JERSEY 08865-0817

ISBN: 978-1-59638-790-4 (pbk)
ISBN: 978-1-59638-791-1 (ePub)
ISBN: 978-1-59638-792-8 (Mobi)

*Page design by Tobias Design*

Printed in the United States of America

**Library of Congress Control Number: 2014938298**

*For Christy, Joshua, and Noah*

# CONTENTS

# FOREWORD

*The New Testament is in the Old concealed;*
*the Old Testament is in the New revealed.*
*—Augustine*

Concerning this salvation, the prophets who prophesied about the grace that was to be yours searched and inquired carefully, inquiring what person or time the Spirit of Christ in them was indicating when he predicted the sufferings of Christ and the subsequent glories. It was revealed to them that they were serving not themselves but you, in the things that have now been announced to you through those who preached the good news to you by the Holy Spirit sent from heaven, things into which angels long to look. (1 Peter 1:10–12)

"Moreover, some women of our company amazed us. They were at the tomb early in the morning, and when they did not find his body, they came back saying that they had even seen a vision of angels, who said that he was alive. Some of those who were with us went to the tomb and found it just as the women had said, but him they did not see." And he said to them, "O foolish ones, and slow of heart to believe all that the prophets have spoken! Was it not necessary that the Christ should suffer these things and enter into his glory?" And beginning with Moses and all the Prophets, he interpreted to them

> in all the Scriptures the things concerning himself. (Luke 24:22–27)

The prophets searched. Angels longed to see. And the disciples didn't understand. But Moses, the Prophets, and all the Old Testament Scriptures had spoken about it—that Jesus would come, suffer, and then be glorified. God began to tell a story in the Old Testament, the ending of which the audience eagerly anticipated. But the Old Testament audience was left hanging. The plot was laid out, but the climax was delayed. The unfinished story begged for an ending. In Christ, God has provided the climax to the Old Testament story. Jesus did not arrive unannounced; his coming was declared *in advance* in the Old Testament—not just in explicit prophecies of the Messiah, but also by means of the stories of all the events, characters, and circumstances in the Old Testament. God was telling a larger, overarching, unified story. From the account of creation in Genesis to the final stories of the return from exile, God progressively unfolded his plan of salvation. And the Old Testament account of that plan always pointed in some way to Christ.

## AIMS OF THIS SERIES

The Gospel According to the Old Testament series was begun by my former professors, Tremper Longman and Al Groves, to whom I owe an enormous personal debt of gratitude. I learned from them a great deal about how to recognize the gospel in the Old Testament. I share their deep conviction that the Bible, both Old and New Testaments, is a unified revelation of God and that its thematic unity is found in Christ. This series of studies will continue to pursue their initial aims:

- to lay out the pervasiveness of the revelation of Christ in the Old Testament

- to promote a Christ-centered reading of the Old Testament
- to encourage Christ-centered preaching and teaching from the Old Testament

These volumes are written primarily for pastors and laypeople, not scholars. They are designed in the first instance to serve the church, not the academy.

My hope and prayer remain the same as Tremper and Al's: that this series will continue to encourage the revival of interest in the Old Testament as a book that constantly points forward to Jesus Christ, to his sufferings and the glories that would follow.

IAIN M. DUGUID

CHAPTER ONE

# READING ESTHER

*Any religion which does not affirm that God is hidden is not true; and any religion which does not offer the reason of it is not instructive. (Blaise Pascal*[1]*)*

Within the Bible, Esther is a story unlike any other, with a charm all its own. "In Esther, unsubtle villains meet with brutal fates; proud partisans are fully vindicated; lovely heroines retain the affection of all; and stolid, dim-witted monarchs are there to be used by all."[2] But Esther is more than just a good story with literary panache; it is also a distinctively theological work, albeit in the subtlest of ways, with an often underappreciated contribution to make to the whole witness of Scripture as a testimony about Christ. Therefore, a consideration of the theological truths the book addresses and of how the book fits into the redemptive story line that culminates in the person and work of Christ provides the proper framework for reading the book profitably.

## READING ESTHER THEOLOGICALLY

Through the centuries, Esther has sometimes been judged as theologically deficient, an opinion that was expressed in the mixed reception it found in the early church. This was not so much because of what it does contain, but more because of what it does not contain. Famously, God is nowhere mentioned in the book. Nor is there any instance of a conspicuous miracle or indisputable divine intervention. Neither is there any mention of prayer, which is especially strange because there is reference to fasting, or any of the other central features of Israelite worship, such as the temple, Jerusalem, or the Torah. Furthermore, there is no mention of the essential marks of faithful living in the postexilic period, such as the observance of dietary laws and injunctions against intermarriage with non-Jews. Thus, the book of Esther appears to be merely a "secular" story of court intrigue in the Persian Empire, without any real involvement of God in the events.

Yet, ironically, it is just this aspect that provides the Christian with the perfect entry point into understanding Esther's distinctive theological contribution. The vast majority of people today will see their own experience in Esther, much more than in many other books of the Bible. Most people today have never experienced a conspicuous miracle or an indisputable divine intervention. Most people today live in a world that looks a lot like Esther's, where events and situations show no obvious or blatant action of God in the midst of them. They show nothing out of the ordinary, nothing miraculous, and nothing overtly supernatural. On the surface, it often appears as if God is absent or hidden from view. Many people look for clues and traces, but find mostly that God is very hard, if not impossible, to find.

As a result, many people, Christians included, simply default into thinking of the world in reductionist, "secular" ways and then go about their lives as if God were not really involved, even if they would never say so out loud. After all, the world really does seem to operate merely according to natural, scientific laws. Events do seem to be driven by historically explainable forces of politics, economics, psychology, and sociology. Life does seem to be governed by human choices and natural processes. By most people's accounting, that is simply how the world works, and because it is, it is also easy to understand how many Christians end up being more or less functional deists, believing that God exists and is "up there," but going about the normal matters of daily life as if he were not really involved much at all.

Nevertheless, we sense that something is wrong with this picture. When the world is viewed mechanistically and we live like functional deists, we inevitably discover that there is a hole in the center, where meaning and life and essence are supposed to be. As Gordon McConville puts it, we live in "a modern world which has become accustomed to explaining things apart from God. We . . . are good at tracing causes and effects, but poor at understanding the meaning of reality."[3] Consequently, most Christians are left with a difficult tension. On the one hand, their world seems to operate without the intervention of God, but on the other hand they do believe that God exists. In the middle of this tension are the same questions that the reader of Esther is forced to ask: Where is God in all of this? Why does it seem as if he is absent? If he is real and present, then why is he so inconspicuous? When life becomes unbearable, when evil is advancing, when suffering becomes intolerable, why doesn't he intervene in noticeable and obvious ways?

For many, such questions have produced doubts, if not an all-out crisis of faith. A few years ago, the journal *Biblical Archaeology Review* held a roundtable discussion with four scholars about how scholarship affects faith. Of the four participants, two had kept their faith and two had lost their faith. In their discussion, one of the scholars who lost his faith put it rather bluntly: "I think that faith has to have substance. But once you start putting some substance onto that, you get into trouble. Faith in the Judeo-Christian tradition has a God who intervenes. That's what the Exodus event is, that's what the crucifixion is: it's a

God who intervenes, and when I look around this world, I don't see a God who intervenes."[4] Certainly many others have lamented the same thing—if not out loud, then at least within the private aches of their own hearts.

Even those who have not given up their faith, as this scholar did, still wrestle with the question, why does God seem so hidden so much of the time? As the philosophers Daniel Howard-Snyder and Paul K. Moser aptly put it,

> Many people are perplexed, even troubled, by the fact that God (if such there be) has not made His existence sufficiently clear. This fact—the fact of divine hiddenness—is a source of existential concern for many people. . . . For many Christians, the difficulty is exacerbated by the fact that their Lord has promised, "Seek, and you will find; knock, and the door will be opened for you" (Matt. 7:7). Having sought and knocked (and knocked again and again), they still fail to find, and no one answers the door for them. . . . Trust in God then crumbles, along with any hope anchored in God's providence. Giving up the struggle to trust the hidden God often seems the only reasonable option as well as the only avenue to psychological well-being. Hence, even devout theists can face an existential crisis from divine hiddenness.[5]

However, it is precisely into this existential crisis provoked by the hiddenness of God and its related theological questions that the book of Esther can speak with a unique voice. Thankfully, God has seen fit to include within the canon of Scripture books that show a range of explicit divine involvement; Esther is on one end of this spectrum. Some parts of Scripture show that God at times works visibly and unmistakably, as in the accounts of Moses, Elijah, and Elisha. Other parts show that God sometimes works behind the scenes in ways that are subtle but perhaps still detectable, as in the narratives of Joseph and Ruth. In still other parts, most notably in Esther, God seems completely absent and inactive.[6] All three are theologically necessary. In a book like Exodus, God assures us that he can and occasionally has intervened in dramatic and unmistakable ways. In a book like Ruth, God assures us that sometimes he works in ways that are only faintly noticeable. However, in a book like Esther, God has given us something that looks a lot like the kind of world most people inhabit: the book of Esther has nothing out of the ordinary, nothing miraculous, and nothing overtly supernatural, and the events unfold with the seeming absence of God and with no detectable trace of his intervention. He simply remains "offstage" and out of view, directing things and working in ways that we cannot see.

In that sense, the book of Esther *is* theological. It is just that the theology is not *on* the surface, but *under* the surface. On the surface, the story is one of conflict between Haman and the Jews. On a deeper level, however, it is a story that evaluates two competing theories of how the world works. On one side is the apparent callousness, injustice, and cruelty of fate, especially embodied in the casting of lots; on the other side is the wise but secret providence of God, embodied in the invisible divine hand (invisible in the events of the book and even in the narrator's portrayal of those events), which is at work even when we cannot see it, do not understand it, and sometimes even doubt it is there. Thus, Esther, perhaps more than any other Old Testament book, shows us that God must be trusted even when he cannot be seen, and that we must learn to live by faith and not by sight. On the surface, the world may look like a senseless unfolding of injustice and fate, but below the surface is the invisible but providential hand of God, orchestrating all things to accomplish his purposes.

The narrator does this through artful literary techniques that subtly hint at God's active presence, despite his apparent absence. The first technique is the use of coincidences. If one encounters one or two coincidences, one might just chalk it up to the fact that sometimes things break in one's favor. But in Esther the sheer number of coincidences and the way in which they become increasingly frequent and incredible as the story progresses eventually begin to defy credibility and leave the reader with the unmistakable impression that something more than serendipity is going on. The story begins with the Persian queen's timely dismissal, which opens the door for Esther's ascent. When a search is begun for a new queen, it "just so happens" that Esther is brought in for the competition; it "just so happens" that she wins the favor of the eunuch in charge; it "just so happens" that Esther finds favor in the eyes of the king. After becoming the queen, it "just so happens" that Mordecai is working in the king's gate and learns of an assassination plot; it "just so happens" that his name is recorded in the king's book of memorable deeds and there is a courtly oversight to reward him properly. When Haman becomes enraged at Mordecai, it "just so happens" that the lot cast to find the best day for the destruction of the Jews falls almost a year away, giving the Jews ample time to prepare for the day. When Esther goes to plead with the king for her people, it "just so happens" that she once again finds favor with him. When she defers her request until the next day, it "just so happens" that Haman crosses paths with Mordecai again and becomes so enraged that he decides to execute him immediately, instead of waiting another eleven months. While the builders are constructing the gallows through the night, it "just so happens" that Haman decides he can't wait any longer and goes to seek the king's permission in the middle of the night. Meanwhile, it "just so happens" that the king cannot sleep, it "just so happens" that the book of memorable deeds is brought in to be read, and it "just so happens" that the reader opens to the spot where Mordecai's good deed is recorded. Immediately after the reading of the court's failure to reward Mordecai, it "just so happens" that Haman shows up. It "just so happens" that the king omits Mordecai's name, allowing Haman to think that the king wants to honor him instead of Mordecai. After the humiliation of having to honor Mordecai, Haman comes to Esther's banquet, where she implicates Haman in the plot to kill her people. When the king leaves in anger and Haman begins to beg Esther for his life, it "just so happens" that the king returns at the exact moment when Haman's pleading looks like an assault on the queen. When the king is further enraged, it "just so happens" that a eunuch points out the presence of gallows newly built, providing the king with a ready-made way to execute Haman. Again, any one coincidence on its own might prove intriguing at best, but the cumulative effect of all the coincidences is to suggest quite strongly that someone is behind the scenes ensuring that events line up in a certain way.

The second technique, which is somewhat related to the first, is the use of peripeteia. In literary terms, peripeteia is the sudden or unexpected reversal of a situation. From beginning to end, the book of Esther is loaded with reversals, both big and small.[7] Examples include Vashti's sudden downfall, complemented by Esther's sudden rise; Esther's fear that she may perish, but finding favor from the king; Haman's joy at being invited to an exclusive banquet with the king and queen, which quickly turns into disgrace; Haman planning to destroy Mordecai, but ending up parading him with honor throughout the city; Haman falling on the queen's couch to plead for mercy being the catalyst for his immediate demise; Haman building gallows to hang Mordecai, but being hung on them instead, while Mordecai takes his position and house; and the Israelites who were doomed to slaughter instead achieving an overwhelming victory.

The third technique, which is much more subtle, is the use of the protagonist's name, which provides a hint of a divine hand that is hidden, yet active. Significantly, the first time Esther is introduced she is identified with two names, not one. Her Hebrew name is *Hadassah*, and her Persian name is *Esther*. In Hebrew, *Hadassah* means "myrtle"; in the Persian world, the name *Esther* is likely related to either the goddess Ishtar or the Persian word for "star." Interestingly enough, Ishtar was the goddess of love and war, two matters in which Esther plays a prominent role in the story. Even more interesting, however, is that when Esther's Persian name is read as a Hebrew word, it means "I am hiding" or "I am hidden." Of course, as the story unfolds, concealment is a major theme.[8] Vashti is deposed because she insists on concealing her body. When a search for a new queen is begun, Esther conceals her Jewish identity. When her people are threatened and she invites the king to a banquet, she conceals her true intentions. She is, as her name suggests, one who hides.

However, in the Jewish rabbinic tradition, Esther's name was more than a clever wordplay revealing her role in the story; it was an indication that the story as a whole was one of hiding—divine hiding. More specifically, the rabbis related the story to the passage in Deuteronomy 31 where God says, "I will surely hide my face."[9] In its original context, the promise in Deuteronomy that God will hide his face is a sign of God's displeasure and judgment, which results in exile. However, it is also a passage that promises that though God may hide his face for a season, he will not allow his people to be destroyed completely. The resonances with the story of Esther are clear. God may hide his face, but that does not mean that he has forsaken his people. As the rabbis perceived, that grand and wonderful truth is writ large in Israel's "macro" story of exile and return. It is writ smaller in Israel's "micro" story of threat and deliverance in Esther, but it is inscribed powerfully and symbolically in the very name of the protagonist herself.

The fourth technique is the use of the third-person omniscient point of view in the narration, such that the reader is implicitly placed in the heavenly viewing room to watch the events unfold while sitting alongside the divine orchestrator. Nowhere is this captured more vividly than in an intriguing passage in the Babylonian Talmud, which relates a rabbinic discussion about which details in the book of Esther demonstrate God's involvement in its authorship. The passage reads,

> Rabbi Eleazar says: Esther was composed under the inspiration of the Holy Spirit, as it says, "And Haman said in his heart." Rabbi Akiba says: Esther was composed under the inspiration of the Holy Spirit, as it says, "And Esther found favour in the eyes of all that looked upon her." Rabbi Meir says, Esther was composed under the inspiration of the Holy Spirit, as it says, "And the thing became known to Mordecai." Rabbi Yose ben Durmaskith said: Esther was composed under the inspiration of the Holy Spirit, as it says, "But on the spoil they laid not their hands."[10]

In other words, the ancient rabbis perceived that the narrative itself, though never mentioning God explicitly, gives all kinds of hints as it goes along that God is involved in the story. After all, how could the narrator know what was in Haman's heart or the private information about which Mordecai became aware or that no one in the entire empire laid his hands on the spoil? Clearly, the Holy Spirit must have been at work, inspiring the recording of the events. From there, it is a reasonable inference that if God's Spirit was present for, and knowledgeable of, all these events, he must have been involved in them as well.

Finally, the book as a whole is written in a way that alludes to an earlier biblical account in Israel's history, which serves to shape the reader's expectation that God is in fact involved in the events of Esther, even if he is nowhere mentioned. As many have noticed, the events in Esther bear a striking similarity to the events in the

Joseph story.[11] Both are set in the court of a foreign ruler, in which they maintain some level of secrecy. In both, the hero rises to prominence inside the court, but then suffers a precipitous decline. In both, the heroes overcome their misfortune, and their resulting rise leads to the deliverance of their people. In both, the turning point comes through the king's disturbed sleep, when he remembers the Israelite. In both, the heroes are rewarded by the bestowal of royal power upon them. In both, there is a royal banquet in which the invited guests (Joseph's brothers, Haman) do not know the true identity of the host/hostess, but which serves as a crucial turning point in the salvation of the people. More incidentally, both stories include two eunuchs who act against the king, both stories contain actions misunderstood as sexual assaults, and both stories involve punishment by hanging.

At times, the correspondence between the two stories comes even closer than similar plot developments. Several passages in Esther are linguistically close to parallel passages in the Joseph story:[12]

| *Genesis 39:10* | *Esther 3:4* |
|---|---|
| And as she spoke to Joseph day after day, he would not listen to her . . . | And when they spoke to him day after day and he would not listen to them . . . |
| *Genesis 41:34–37* | *Esther 2:3–4* |
| Let Pharaoh proceed to appoint overseers over the land . . . and let them gather all the food of these good years. . . . This proposal pleased Pharaoh and all his servants. | And let the king appoint officers in all the provinces of his kingdom to gather all the beautiful young virgins. . . . This pleased the king, and he did so. |

| *Genesis 41:42–43* | *Esther 6:11* |
|---|---|
| Then Pharaoh took his signet ring from his hand and put it on Joseph's hand, and clothed him in garments of fine linen and put a gold chain about his neck. And he made him ride in his second chariot. And they called out before him, "Bow the knee!" Thus he set him over all the land of Egypt. | So Haman took the robes and the horse, and he dressed Mordecai and led him through the square of the city, proclaiming before him, "Thus shall it be done to the man whom the king delights to honor." |
| *Genesis 44:34* | *Esther 8:6* |
| For how can I go back to my father if the boy is not with me? I fear to see the evil that would find my father. | For how can I bear to see the calamity that is coming to my people? Or how can I bear to see the destruction of my kindred? |

There may also be some similarities in phrasing, if not quite as strong, between Genesis 40:20 and Esther 1:3; 2:18; Genesis 44:24 and Esther 8:6; Genesis 43:31; 45:1 and Esther 5:10; and Genesis 50:3 and Esther 2:12. The point, however, is that the attentive reader will naturally pick up a series of echoes from the Joseph story that will serve to frame the Esther story in a similar light. In the Joseph story, God's role was made explicit: "As for you, you meant evil against me, but God meant it for good, to bring it about that many people should be kept alive, as they are today" (Gen. 50:20). Given all the similarities between the two stories, the reader naturally expects the role of God to be the same in Esther, only implicit instead of explicit.

Taken together, the use of a whole range of literary techniques—coincidences, peripeteia, naming, point of view, and allusion—skillfully marks the book of Esther as a story of God's "absent presence" and his "hidden involvement." On the surface, he appears to be absent and uninvolved; in reality, however, under the surface, he is providentially at work to accomplish his purposes and to deliver his people. Theologically, that is the distinctive contribution of the book of Esther. As Barry Webb writes,

> How does the "absence" of God colour the theme of deliverance in the book of Esther and contribute to its distinctive theology? . . . [It shows that] God is present even when he is most absent; when there are no miracles, dreams, or visions, no charismatic leaders, no prophets to interpret what is happening, and not even any explicit God-talk. And he is present as deliverer. Those whom he saved by signs and wonders at the exodus he continues to save through his hidden, providential control of their history. His people are never at the mercy of blind fate or of malign powers, whether human or supernatural.[13]

It needs to be emphasized that this providential mercy is true for the Jews in Esther not simply because they are the fortunate beneficiaries of a generic providence. It is true for them because—and only because—God refuses to allow the destruction of his special covenant people. Of course, God's providence involves and touches all people and all nations, for good or for ill. But the powerful testimony of Esther is that God works out his providential designs for the benefit of his chosen people, for the simple reason that they are *his chosen covenant people*. In that sense, the testimony of God's hidden providence in Esther is an extended Old Testament example of Paul's famous line,

"We know that for those who love God all things work together for good, for those who are called according to his purpose" (Rom. 8:28).

One consequence of this realization is that the message of Esther and the larger theological problem of divine hiddenness can be understood only as they are related to God's covenant promises and commitments; and that, of course, is simply another way of saying that they can be understood fully only in light of the person and work of Christ, who is the climax of God's covenant and the fulfillment of all his promises.

## READING ESTHER CHRISTOLOGICALLY

To understand how Christ relates to the book of Esther and the theological questions to which it speaks, the reader needs to appreciate how Christ is the simultaneous fulfillment of two different trajectories.

First, *Christ is the ultimate revelation of God's hidden presence in the world*. In the Old Testament, God is both present and absent. For instance, God is present in a powerful and personal way with Abraham. When Moses is tending his flocks in Midian, God speaks to him from within the burning bush. After delivering Israel from Egypt and bringing the people to Mount Sinai, God speaks directly to Moses from the mountain. When Joshua is preparing to lead the people into the Promised Land, God assures him, "Just as I was with Moses, so I will be with you. I will not leave you or forsake you" (Josh. 1:5).

Yet, at the same time, God also hides himself. To Moses he says,

> I will forsake them and hide my face from them, and they will be devoured. . . . And I will surely hide my face in that day because of all the evil that they have done. (Deut. 31:17–18; see also Deut. 32:20)

Later in Israel's history, the prophet Isaiah confesses during the Assyrian crisis,

> I will wait for the LORD, who is hiding his face from the house of Jacob, and I will hope in him. (Isa. 8:17)

In the Psalms, others make similar statements, though with more lament than hope:

> Why, O LORD, do you stand far away?
> Why do you hide yourself in times of trouble?
> (Ps. 10:1)
>
> How long, O LORD? Will you forget me forever?
> How long will you hide your face from me? (Ps. 13:1)
>
> My God, my God, why have you forsaken me?
> Why are you so far from saving me, from the words of my groaning? (Ps. 22:1)
>
> Why do you hide your face?
> Why do you forget our affliction and oppression?
> (Ps. 44:24)
>
> But I, O LORD, cry to you;
> in the morning my prayer comes before you.
> O LORD, why do you cast my soul away?
> Why do you hide your face from me?
> Afflicted and close to death from my youth up,
> I suffer your terrors; I am helpless. (Ps. 88:13–15)

These cries could perhaps be dismissed as merely the exclamations of souls in pain or the natural experience of judgment for sin, yet elsewhere divine hiddenness is actually said to be part of the very nature and essence of who God is: "Truly, you are a God who hides himself, O God of Israel" (Isa. 45:15).

Even more intriguingly, as the Old Testament unfolds, there is a gradual shift from presence to absence. It is as if God slowly disappears and recedes from perceptible involvement as history progresses.[14] As the Bible opens its story, God is intimately involved and accessible to the first human beings. He walks in the garden of Eden, and the first couple can hear and understand his voice. Even after they sin, God comes looking for them and they are able to have an actual conversation with him. In subsequent events, as when Noah builds the ark or the builders construct the Tower of Babel, God is still involved and easily discernible, though a little less so than with Adam and Eve. By the time we come to Abraham, a new expression emerges. For the first time, God is said to "appear," meaning "is seen." His appearance comes through a fire in the midst of a dream, which is a slightly more remote engagement than before.

For the generation of the exodus, God is clearly present, with divinely powerful manifestations. At Sinai, they hear the divine voice and see the divine fire, and they become utterly paralyzed with fear. In fact, they beg Moses not to let God speak with them directly, lest they die; instead, they want him to relay to them what he says. From this point on, prophets will be intermediaries for communication with God. From then on, God will speak to the people through his prophets, not directly. And so, in the subsequent generations, God's presence slowly begins to withdraw—no pillar of cloud and fire, no more manna, no fantastic visible manifestations of glory, only some sporadic miracles.

But miracles become fewer and farther between as well. At the beginning of 1 Samuel there are a few miracles, but there are hardly any by the end of the book and almost none at all in 2 Samuel. From there, God's presence continues to recede, step by step. Samuel is the last person to whom God is said to have been revealed. Solomon is the last person to whom God is said to have appeared. Elijah is the last person through whom God does a public miracle, bringing down the fire on the altar at Mount Carmel. In the next chapter, a major shift occurs. God declares that he will no longer be found in dramatic manifestations like wind, earthquakes, and fire, but will be heard only in "the sound of a low whisper" (1 Kings 19:12), the still small voice, or even better, in the sound of silence. As it turns out, this is the last time in the Old Testament story that the text says that "the Lord said" anything to anyone. About a century later, Hezekiah asks for the shadow on the steps to back up, and that is the last miracle in the Old Testament narrative. The last instance of an angel acting upon the earth occurs shortly thereafter, when an angel routs the Assyrian troops overnight in order to deliver Jerusalem. The only appearance of angels from then on is in dreams or visions. All that is left of God's presence is in the temple, and when that is destroyed by the Babylonians, there is one last mention of fire. Ironically, it is not the fire of God's presence anymore, but the fire of his judgment. Ezekiel notes that his glory departs, and that is the end of that.

In the postexilic period, the narrative has a decidedly different tone. In books like Ezra and Nehemiah, there are no miracles or angels or divine manifestations. There is no record that God spoke directly to anyone. The book of Esther stands at the end of the narrative, and in Esther God is not even mentioned at all. By this point, God has completely receded from view. Everything would seem to indicate that people are on their own, left to their own resources to make their way through the world.

As a result, there is a kind of tension that has developed between the reality of God's seeming absence and the belief in God's abiding presence. What was able to hold these two things together was faith in the promises of God. As Samuel Terrien nicely summarizes it,

> Faded presence became a memory and a hope, but it burnt into an alloy of inward certitude, which was . . . "faith." When God no longer overwhelmed

> the senses of perception and concealed himself behind the adversity of historical existence, those who accepted the promise were still aware of God's nearness in the very veil of his seeming absence. For them, the center of life was a *Deus absconditus atque praesens* [God hidden but present].[15]

Jesus, however, is the resolution of the tension, and he resolves the tension not by explaining the mystery of simultaneous presence and absence but by embodying both of them at the same time. In Jesus, paradoxically, the hidden God is revealed *and* the revealed God is hidden.

On the one hand, the hidden God is revealed. In Jesus, God is made manifest in the flesh. Angels announce his coming. Miracles punctuate his ministry. God speaks through him and in him, for he is quite literally the Word made flesh. In him, God is with us in the most radical and demonstrative way, for he is Immanuel, "God with us." Thus, Jesus is the final and greatest revelation of God, the one in whom the hidden God has been made manifest. That is, he represents God's presence to us.

Yet, on the other hand, in Jesus the revealed God is hidden. In one sense, this is because in Jesus, God is in the world but frequently goes unrecognized. People dismiss him as insane or even evil (Mark 3:20–22), failing to recognize (or acknowledge) who he truly is. God is in their midst, and yet they cannot (or will not) see it.

But, in another sense, and even more profoundly, Jesus enters into our experience and thus experiences the absence of God himself. That is, just as he represents God's presence *to* us, he also experiences God's absence *for* us. When Jesus dies on the cross, he takes upon his own lips the cry of the psalmist, that agonizing and terrifying reality that God has receded and hidden his face: "My God, my God, why have you forsaken me?" (Matt. 27:46; Mark 15:34).

That God would take on human flesh and, even more scandalously, that God would die in the flesh puts him completely out of reach of our rational human thinking.[16] Divine incarnation and divine crucifixion are the boldest expressions of God's own statement, "For my thoughts are not your thoughts, neither are your ways my ways, declares the LORD. For as the heavens are higher than the earth, so are my ways higher than your ways and my thoughts than your thoughts" (Isa. 55:8). Thus, in taking on human flesh in the womb of Mary and in dying on the cross, God not only reveals himself but, in a very real sense, conceals himself. That is, by revealing himself in such a shocking, unexpected, and scandalous way, God shrouds himself from anyone who will not seek to understand him through faith. As one New Testament scholar puts it, in summarizing Martin Luther's view,

> The suffering, failure, and abandonment exhibited at Calvary is [*sic*] the quintessential instance of a revelation wherein God is most magnificently unveiled while remaining utterly hidden. God is hidden in the cross, not because the crucifixion falsifies or obscures any part of his character, but because the truth revealed in a crucified Savior is inaccessible to anyone who will not look through the eyes of faith. Faith alone is able to perceive the truth lodged in this apparent contradiction, not because it believes the irrational but because it is willing to yield before the unexpected, to surrender to the unacceptable.[17]

Thus, in Jesus the tension is resolved, and it is resolved because it is embodied. He embodies it in a way in which the *Deus absconditus atque praesens* becomes a reality—not an abstract reality or a philosophical reality, but a *personal* reality. That is profoundly significant because a personal reality is not a philosophical solution to a philosophical problem (how can God be God and yet be so hidden?), but a person to be trusted. Since Jesus is the personal embodiment of God's presence made real within the world and at the same time the embodiment of our experience of God's seeming absence within the world, then it is through him—and only through him—that we are able to begin to understand God's ways in the world and with us.

So, in the end, we are back not only to the analogous experience of those in the Old Testament who struggled and grappled with the hiddenness of God, but also to the means by which they navigated the struggle: faith in what has already been revealed and faith in the promises that have been made. In short, the only way to make sense of a world in which God seems so absent so much of the time is to look to Christ in faith. This means to look at the mystery of the incarnation and the shock of the crucifixion and to see the world through the lens of the one who is the presence of God to us and who, in solidarity with us, has entered into the seeming absence of God for us, all at the same time.

Moreover, what is true for the broad theological issue of divine hiddenness is also true more particularly for the book of Esther, which is the narrative example *par excellence* of that very issue in the Bible. Thus, Christ is not only the ultimate revelation of God's hidden presence in the world, but Christ is also *the ultimate embodiment of God's particular pattern of deliverance in Esther.* Sadly, this has not always been appreciated. Early on in church history, the hanging of Haman was frequently identified with the crucifixion of Christ, particularly by Jews trying to emphasize the scandal of the cross.[18] A few church fathers picked up on the suggestion as part of their polemics, but the proposed identification between Christ and Haman seems to have "spoiled the typological well" for many, so that the correspondences between Esther and Christ were overlooked.

But this is unfortunate, because the narrative shape of God's salvation through Esther bears a striking correspondence to the shape of God's salvation through Jesus. In the book of Esther, a royal figure takes upon herself the plight of her people, faces a life-threatening peril on their behalf, and because of her faithfulness brings about the salvation of her people. As a result, the people are filled with joy and celebrate their victory over evil and death with great feasting. The very same pattern is seen in Jesus. He is a royal figure who takes upon himself the plight of his people. He too faces a life-threatening (indeed, a life-ending) peril on their behalf. He too brings about the salvation of his people through his faithfulness. And, as a result, his people too are filled with joy and celebrate their victory over evil and death with great feasting.

Not only the narrative shapes of the two correspond to each other, but also the way in which both Esther and Christ act as representatives for their people. Just as all the Jews faced death because of the act of one man, so in a similar way all humanity faces death because of the act of one man (Rom. 5:12, 15, 19). But, just as all God's people were saved through the faithful act of Esther, so all God's people are saved through the faithful act of Christ (Rom. 5:15, 18–19).

Once one enters into the details of the story, even more typological connections reveal themselves. Many of these will be developed in the following chapters, but already it is clear that Esther serves as a typological figure who points us ahead to the person and work of Christ on behalf of his people.

Thus, Esther is a story that cannot merely be brushed aside as a secular story of intrigue within the Persian court; it is so much more than that. It is a glorious story of God's providential and redemptive work in the world despite his apparent absence (at times), a work that comes to its fullest embodiment and expression in the glorious story of Jesus. As such, the book of Esther has a rightful place in the canon of Scripture, in the whole counsel of God, and in the theological reflections of the Christian on divine hiddenness. For all three, its contribution is both indispensible and invaluable.

## FOR FURTHER REFLECTION

1. In what ways have you struggled personally and spiritually with God's seeming absence in your life?
2. How have you sought to make sense of it?
3. How does Jesus help us to make sense of divine hiddenness in our own lives? What might a Christ-focused response look like when God seems to be absent?

CHAPTER TWO

# WILL THE REAL KING PLEASE STAND UP? (1:1–22)

*Who enjoy the purest and most genuine pleasure; is it they who recline for a full day on couches, and join breakfast and dinner together, and distend their stomach, and blunt their senses? (John Chrysostom*[1]*)*

The book of Esther begins with a historical notice indicating that the events are set during the days of the Persian ruler Ahasuerus, otherwise known as Xerxes I, who ruled the Persian Empire (sometimes called the Achaemenid Persian Empire) from 486 until 465 B.C.[2] During this period, the Persian Empire was the dominant power in the ancient Near East, with territory extending across most of the known world. However, early in Ahasuerus's reign, an Egyptian revolt erupted, followed closely by two rebellions in Babylon. These insurrections were crushed decisively, but the real challenge came from Greece. Ahasuerus's father, Darius, had struggled against the Greeks during what was known as the First Persian War (492–490 B.C.), but it was left to Ahasuerus to lead a second invasion of Greece (480–479 B.C.), which resulted in the subjugation of several Greek cities before a string of costly defeats stopped the Persian advance.[3]

## THE ROYAL BANQUETS (1:1–9)

Since the events at the beginning of Esther took place in the third year of Ahasuerus's reign, they must be set in the time after the Egyptian and Babylonian revolts, but before the invasion of Greece, when Ahasuerus was in his mid-thirties. At this point in his reign, as the narrator notes, he was in control of 127 provinces stretching from India in the east to the upper Nile region in the west. The narrator could have simply noted the number of satrapies within the empire (a satrapy is a regional area that encompasses several provinces), of which there were never more than thirty-one, but opting for the larger number more clearly impresses upon the reader the extensive scope and power of the empire over which Ahasuerus was king. In fact, the Persian Empire was so vast and so powerful that it had four capital cities. One of them was Susa, a city situated on a fertile plain about 150 miles north of the Persian Gulf, near the modern-day border of Iran and Iraq. The crown jewel of the city was the royal palace, which sat high on a mound on the west side of the city and was typically a winter or spring residence for the king. Still, due to its location, Susa was almost unbearably hot during much of the year, and the royal palace was therefore built with a garden portico, which allowed for cross breezes to make the residents more comfortable.[4]

It is in this palace, according to the book of Esther, that Ahasuerus throws a huge feast of celebration in the third year of his reign. Whether he does so to celebrate the recent military victories over Egypt and Babylon or to celebrate his recent marriage is left unstated. However, it must be a time of relative peace in order for the king to be able to feast for six months. In any case, Ahasuerus, no stranger to excess and indulgence, throws a 180-day feast for his military leaders, the nobles, and the governors of the empire's provinces. Afterward, Ahasuerus throws another banquet for all the male citizens of Susa. This seven-day banquet, like the six-month feast, is probably more like a frat party than anything else. In fact, the Hebrew term for "banquet" is related to the word for "drinking"—and rightly so.[5] Most Persian banquets were something akin to an ancient keg party.

The narrator then gives a jaw-dropping description of the royal grounds. In fact, this is the only place in the Old Testament where a narrator describes in such detail the background environment of a scene.[6] The reason, presumably, is to give the reader a sense of just how opulent and lavish these feasts are. The garden portico has beautiful, hanging drapes made of white and blue materials. At the top, they are fitted with silver rods that fasten them onto grand marble pillars. Around them are royal cords made of white and purple material. Around the portico are luxuriant couches fashioned from gold and silver. The floor shows exquisite mosaic tile work, made out of porphyry, marble, mother-of-pearl, and other expensive material. Those in attendance are drinking wine out of golden goblets. In Persian culture, the variety of goblets was a sign of wealth, and here no two goblets are the same; each one is a unique artistic creation. And each man holding a goblet can drink as much as he desires. The wording of the edict is that there is to be no compulsion, which apparently means that everyone can drink when and how much he wishes—somewhat ironically mandating that everyone drink without restriction.[7] Clearly, the expectation is that everyone will drink without scruple or reserve. In fact, everything about the banquet, from the abundance of wine to the luxuriant decor, speaks of extravagance, excess, ostentation, and indulgence. Meanwhile, Ahasuerus's wife, Queen Vashti, also throws a great feast for all the women inside the palace.

There is, in all these elaborate descriptions, a characterization of the king. He is portrayed as someone who has extravagant wealth, unlimited power, and unrivaled pretension. Noblemen, military officials, wineries, stone masons, interior decorators, and furniture craftsmen are under his command. The wealth of the kingdom is at his disposal, and he thinks nothing of lavishly parading it in front of those under him. He possibly puts on his full display of pride, pomp, and power to reassure his people that he has the resources to defeat the Greeks. Even the simple, one-verse description of the queen's banquet, compared to the elaborate description of the king's banquet, acts as a literary foil, highlighting the excessiveness of the king and his party. Clearly, Ahasuerus lacks nothing and spares nothing.

The contrast with the plight of the Jews could not have been sharper. The Persians were strong; the Jews were weak. The Persians were wealthy; the Jews were poor. The Persians seemed to own the world; the Jews seemed to be passed around from empire to empire. Ahasuerus could do whatever he wished; the Jews could not. In such a situation, the natural theological question to be asked is, "Ahasuerus is on his throne; but is God on his? And if he is, then why don't we see any evidence of it? Why does he seem so absent in the face of world events? Why does he seem so silent?" After all, Israel's history was full of accounts in which God had intervened in world events for the good of his people. He had provided for their forefathers when they were aliens in a strange land. He had delivered the people when they were enslaved in Egypt. He had led them through the Red Sea and given them a land flowing with milk and honey. When challenged, he had worked through prophets like Elijah and Elisha to demonstrate his miraculous power over false gods and pagan powers. The dead were raised, armies of heavenly chariots were camped out on the hills, and fire came down from heaven on an altar at Mount Carmel.

However, that was not the world that the Jews of the Persian Empire knew. In their world, God was silent, but they could hear the sounds spilling down the western mount of Susa when the king threw his banquets in his royal gardens. In their world, God seemed absent, but the Persian political and military machine seemed almost ubiquitous. In their world, they could look up to heaven, but only to see the royal acropolis in Susa looking back down on them and casting a long shadow upon their lives.

## THE QUEEN'S REFUSAL (1:10–12)

On the seventh day, when the king has become "merry with wine," as the narrator describes it, Ahasuerus calls in the seven eunuchs who serve him and commands them to bring Vashti to the party. Having shown off his enormous wealth, he apparently now wants to show off his wife as well. In his eyes, she is a mere possession, a trophy wife to parade in front of the drunken, lecherous men, so that he can take some self-indulgent pride as he watches them gawk at her. According to Persian custom, such an action would normally have been taken only with a concubine.[8] For a Persian queen to be seen like that would have been insulting and scandalous. The king, however, is rash and full of himself, so he makes the impulsive decision to dress his wife up in her royal garb and parade her in front of the inebriated crowd for his and others' pleasure. But the queen has more self-respect than to allow herself to be dehumanized by her drunken husband. As Jeffrey Cohen writes, "Queen Vashti . . . must have been a rare woman to have retained her sense of dignity and morality to the extent that she was prepared to endanger her life by refusing her lord and master's bidding to show off her body to the assembled throng."[9] She refuses to go out into the garden portico and strut around as eye candy for the drunken men of Susa.

## THE KING'S REACTION (1:12–22)

The irony is comical. Every man in the capital city comes to the king's banquet, but his own wife will not. As a result, Ahasuerus becomes furious and burns with anger. However, instead of dealing with the situation in a personal way (after all, she is his wife!), he makes it a public affair by summoning the best legal experts in the empire to figure out what to do with such an "imperial crisis." He makes a family matter into a matter of state, as if a modern-day CEO learned that his son was given a detention at school and called an emergency meeting of the board of directors to determine how to handle the situation when he got home. The king was foolish to summon Vashti in the first place; now he is equally foolish in summoning the legal experts.

When the wise men arrive and are briefed on the "crisis," one of them, a prince named Memucan, suggests that if word gets out that Vashti has defied the king, it will spark a feminist uprising within the empire. The women of the empire will take inspiration from the queen's defiance of the king and act similarly toward their own husbands. The whole order of the empire, he concludes, will be destabilized. Of course, all the advisers no doubt have their own wives in mind as well and certainly recoil at the prospect of being treated contemptuously themselves. After all, if the king can't get his wife to submit to his demands, then what is to stop their own wives from standing up to them in the same way? Therefore, Memucan advises the king to draft a royal decree stating that Vashti is banned from entering the king's presence and that a new queen will be chosen.[10] Then he advises him to send it out to the rest of the empire, urging everyone to maintain the current domestic order. Sadly, in counseling the king in this way, Memucan has done exactly what the king himself did—he has taken a domestic issue and turned it into an empire-wide crisis.

In several ways, this episode is both humorous and ironic. First, the king has asked for legal advice, but instead is given advice solely based on pragmatic concerns—the second time he has asked for something and not been given what he requested, though his reaction is anything but consistent. When he requested Vashti's presence and did not receive it, he exploded with anger; however, when he requests legal advice from his counselors and does not receive it, he is pleased. Second, the advised punishment is no different than what Queen Vashti has already decided for herself. She does not want to come into the presence of the king. Her punishment? She cannot come into the presence of the king! Third, the counselors have been summoned because the king cannot control his wife with a decree. Their advice? Try to control all the women in the empire with a decree! Finally, the counselors are terrified that word of what Vashti has done will get out to the rest of the women in the empire. Their solution? Send out a royal order to all the provinces of the empire, informing everyone what Vashti has done!

None of this, apparently, occurs to Ahasuerus. To him the suggestion is a sound one, and he does exactly as Memucan counsels. He sends letters to all the royal provinces, informing the people of the empire in their native tongues that Vashti has been deposed, that a new queen will be chosen to take her place, and that all women in the empire are to give due honor to their husbands. Little does Ahasuerus know that the queen he will get in Vashti's place will not just refuse him, but will end up completely controlling him! But he will be just as oblivious then as he is now.

## THE SUBTLE AND HIDDEN KING

The scene is resoundingly comical and full of irony and satire, which of course is the point. The Persian elite and especially King Ahasuerus come off looking like a bunch of wine-guzzling buffoons. They drink too much and think too little. They have the whole world at their fingertips, but cannot seem to get things right. They are overly indulgent, yet in the end cannot seem to get what they want. If the Jews in Susa were tempted to think that Ahasuerus was on the throne and that was the end of that, then perhaps this stinging piece of satire should have made them reconsider. Ahasuerus may appear to sit atop the world. He may be able with the snap of a finger to engage a vast, efficient bureaucratic machine. He may have the power of the world's strongest military. He may possess the most advanced communication system, which he can use at will for his own petty purposes. But the one thing that becomes painfully clear in this episode is that he is not nearly as in control as he might think he is. The subtle point of the whole satirical episode is that ultimately Ahasuerus is not really the king of the world after all—God is. God is the one who truly sits on *the* throne.

Within the larger context of the Old Testament, the comparisons between the two kings become even more suggestive. In earlier Old Testament books, God is regularly portrayed as the king of the whole world, and his control and authority extend over all things. His dwelling place is the tabernacle/temple, which is described in thorough and exquisite detail, with an interior that is patterned after a garden. According to the prophets, one day all the peoples of the world will stream to Jerusalem, his imperial city, to feast with him, the king of the world. Similarly, in this episode, Ahasuerus is portrayed as the king of the whole realm, and his control and authority extend over all things in his world-dominating empire. His dwelling place is a palace, which is described in thorough and exquisite detail. (Indeed, the only two buildings in the entire Old Testament that are given such an elaborate description of their furnishings are the tabernacle/temple and Ahasuerus's palace.) It even contains an exquisite garden. (The only two gardens in the Old Testament are found in this part of the world: the garden of Eden, upon which the tabernacle/temple artistry is based, and Ahasuerus's garden.) At the king's invitation, all the peoples of the empire stream to his imperial city to feast with him, the king of the whole empire. The cumulative effect of the thematic parallels subtly sets up God, his temple, his garden, and his banquet for all the peoples over against Ahasuerus, his palace, his garden, and his banquet for all the peoples.[11]

But they are not of the same order. God is the true king; King Ahasuerus is merely a parody of him. God's kingdom is the true kingdom; Persia and every other kingdom are merely parodies of his kingdom. As a result, comparatively speaking, the largest and most powerful regimes in the world are ultimately silly—even comical—in light of God's power and sovereignty.[12] Even in the inner politics of the Persian court, God is acting; he is already orchestrating things to fall into their proper place, and all of it for a greater purpose, namely, so that Esther can make her way onto the scene. And that is the point of the story: the Persian king is flamboyant, but ultimately out of control; God is subtle—indeed, very subtle—but ultimately in control, in *complete* control.

Nowhere is that in sharper relief than in the life of Jesus in the shadow of the mighty Roman Empire, an empire that was not just a vast political entity, but one that embodied a distinct, imperial ideology.[13] Beginning with Augustus's attempt to solidify his political position by declaring that Julius Caesar, his adopted father, had been divinized after his death, it became customary for emperors to make similar assertions about their predecessors and thus be able to claim for themselves the appellation "son of God." Along with this, particularly in the eastern part of the empire, came the establishment of the state cult, which celebrated the divinity of the emperor. In other words, much like Ahasuerus and the Persian Empire, the Roman Empire centuries later had similar kinds of wealth, power, and prestige, with similar self-indulgent excesses.

In Luke's gospel, the birth of Christ contains many of the same themes as Esther 1. It is not insignificant that this account also begins with a notice of who the ruling powers are: Augustus Caesar is on the throne, and Quirinius is the governor of Syria, a reminder of the imperial powers that be (Luke 2:1–2). Here too a decree is issued from the throne, this one compelling everyone to report to his own town to be registered. Since Joseph belongs to the house and family of David, he and his betrothed, Mary, have to make the journey from Nazareth to Bethlehem. After the birth of Jesus, an angel appears and announces, "For unto you is born this day in the city of David a Savior, who is Christ the Lord" (Luke 2:11). A more counter-imperial statement could not have been made. David is referenced three times in the narrative, highlighting again and again that Jesus is from royal stock, born in a royal city. Because Caesar had brought the known world under the hegemony of Rome, he was often heralded as the "Savior" of the world, but the angel says, "No, this child is the true Savior." Because Caesar sat on the throne, ruling over all, he was proclaimed as Lord, but the angel says, "No, this baby lying in his manger is the true Lord." Because Rome dictated the ultimate terms of life in the empire, there was a raw hope among the Jews that God would send the Messiah to liberate his people from Rome's dominion, but now the angel says, "Yes, your hopes have been fulfilled. The Christ has been born."

However, Jesus was Savior, Christ, and Lord in an unexpected way. Instead of toppling the empire, he lived faithfully within it, challenging it when it was necessary, but not picking fights when it wasn't. Eventually, however, the empire would tolerate him no longer and crushed him by nailing him to a cross, with the cruel sign over his head mocking his claim to be the true king and treating him as if *he* were the parody. However, the resurrection three days later demonstrated that the empire would not have the last word; eventually God's kingdom, with Christ as King, would bring all the empires of the world, whether the Persians, the Romans, or any other, to their knees. One day the voices in heaven will declare, "The kingdom of the world has become the kingdom of our Lord and of his Christ, and he shall reign forever and ever" (Rev. 11:15).

But in the meantime, the early Christians needed to be reminded of God's subtle providence in their own lives, which were also lived under the shadow of the empire. The apostle Paul maintained, much like the narrator in Esther, that the wealthy and powerful empire was not the true kingdom, but merely a parody of that kingdom; and Caesar was not the true Lord, but merely a parody of that Lord. Indeed, Paul had come to realize that God was the true king of the world, and that through the birth, life, death, and resurrection of Christ, the kingdom of God had come and was beginning to take over the world. That placed everyone in the position of having to choose between the old, visible order represented by Caesar and his empire, and the new, albeit invisible, order to be found in Christ and his kingdom. Thus, when Paul wrote to the Christians in Philippi, a Roman colony, he reminded them that their real citizenship was in heaven and that from there they awaited in faith their Savior and Lord, Jesus Christ (Phil. 3:20–21). The implicit claim was that their Roman citizenship should take a backseat to their heavenly citizenship. Caesar's claims to be Savior and Lord were hollow, and these titles really belonged to Jesus. The Roman Empire was ultimately a sham, and the true kingdom to which they should be loyal was the kingdom of God.

Even more pointed is Paul's letter to the Romans. As those living right under Caesar's nose, the Roman Christians would have been as aware as anyone of the power and wealth of the empire. Like the Jews in Susa, they lived in the constant shadow of the ruler of the known world. Yet, just as Luke begins his birth narrative, so Paul begins his letter to them with a greeting loaded with counter-imperial language (Rom. 1:1–6). Christ, not Caesar, is the true Son of God. Christ, as the descendant of David, is the true claimant to the throne. Christ, not the emperor, is alone worthy to summon us to the obedience of faith and to command our undivided allegiance. Christ's kingdom, not the Roman Empire, is the true possessor of the nations.

Christians today need the same reminder. The world often seems to be controlled by the powerful and the wealthy, by military might and political prowess. Just like the Jews in the Persian period, we often see the kings of the earth do as they wish. Dictators and tyrants around the world live in opulent luxury, while many of their people live in squalor and poverty. Military powers exert themselves on the helpless, giving more credence to the frustrated complaints that in our world might seems to make right. Political machinery is always working, covering up scandals, making unethical deals, and disguising ulterior agendas. Heartless business executives and Wall Street tycoons make decisions that line their own pockets while simultaneously emptying those in the rank and file of their companies.

Meanwhile, many people look helplessly to the heavens, wondering why God will not intervene. They wonder if the world is really just steered by the wills of the world's rulers. After all, like the Jews in Susa, that is all they can see. In their hearts, though they might not say it, they privately wonder whether God is involved at all and whether there is any point in continuing to trust him in a world where an Ahasuerus or a Caesar sits on the throne. And even if they do find it within themselves to continue to trust him in some sense, they secretly doubt whether it actually makes that much difference in the end, given the seemingly insurmountable and very visible power of a Susa or a Rome.

The temptation is to give up on the invisible kingdom of God, inaugurated by Jesus and coming with force at the end of history, and to acquiesce to the imperial ideologies that press down upon us. It is easy to see the military power of "the empire" and to give in to the tempting thought that might makes right, that brute power is the way to get things done. It is easy to see the materialistic opulence of the American way of life, full of excesses and indulgences akin to the Persian court, and give in to the temptation that the accumulation of luxuries and pleasures is the best way to live in the world. It is easy to see the corruption in business and politics and to resign oneself to the conclusion that such is the way to get things done, and to join in lest one fall behind in life. In short, when we see the world seemingly in the grip of the powers that be, it is all too easy to be carried along with their ideologies, to believe their lies, and to allow ourselves to be shaped by their claims and promises.

But the author of Esther encourages us to see our world instead with the eyes of faith and to understand that those things can never bring us life; like all imperial ideologies, they are doomed in the end. They are merely "banquets in the grave"—no less pathetic than the Persian banquet, when seen from an eternal perspective.[14] Instead, we need to see our world with the eyes of faith, through the lens of Jesus—his life, death, and resurrection—to know that God is always at work, positioning things in the world and in individual lives, even if we cannot see it. Behind the scenes, God is orchestrating all things to serve his greater purposes, even when it means that crosses must come before resurrections.

In truth, the kings of the earth are not really as powerful as they seem. In fact, they are, like the satirized buffoonery of Ahasuerus, silly and comical compared to the Sovereign One who controls all things. That is true whether we can see it or not, whether we recognize it or not. On the surface, it may appear that God is not working anywhere in the world, but the truth is that he is working everywhere, even while the kings of the world wield their scepters, completely oblivious to the God who wields his.

One of Rembrandt's most famous paintings is *The Night Watch*. It hangs in the Rijksmuseum in Amsterdam. In fact, the top floor of the museum is built with a long corridor that leads the visitor into a room at the end where *The Night Watch* hangs, almost as if enthroned in the museum. The painting is itself enormous, thirteen feet by sixteen feet, and many gather to admire it. Imagine walking into the room and standing behind two art lovers having a conversation, one a student and one his much older teacher. After admiring the painting for a while, the teacher asks the student to find Rembrandt in the painting. The student naturally looks in the corners and discovers that there is no signature. Next, he begins looking at the faces. Rembrandt was known for painting his own face into his paintings, but to the student's disappointment he cannot recognize Rembrandt's face in any of the characters in the painting. He continues looking closer at the details of the painting. Perhaps there is some clue, some way that Rembrandt has visibly put himself into the painting. After some time, the exasperated student turns to his teacher and says, "I've looked everywhere in this painting, and nowhere do I see him." Continuing to stare admiringly at the painting, the teacher softly says, "You look for a signature, but I see the subtlety of artistic style. You look at their faces, but I see the character of the brushstrokes. And that is why you look at the painting and conclude the artist is nowhere. And that is why I look at the painting and see the artist everywhere."[15]

The comical satire of Ahasuerus encourages us to do the same. It would be easy to read the episode and look only at the characters or only at the events involving them and, not seeing the name of God anywhere, not having any direct or explicit testimony of his involvement, to conclude that it is just the salacious intrigue of a Persian king and his nobles. It would be easy to conclude that God is nowhere in this story or in the events that form it. Even today we might look at the events of our own lives and see only the people. We might see only the common and ordinary events. And in the absence of any obvious, visible action of God, we might conclude that God is nowhere. But the narrator of the book of Esther, the master teacher, stands next to us and asks, "Where is God in the world today?" And if we listen carefully, we will also hear him whispering, "Look again, but this time with the eyes of faith and you will see: he is everywhere."

## FOR FURTHER REFLECTION

1. In what ways does our world today seem to be controlled by the powerful and the wealthy? How do most people cope with that reality?
2. In what ways have you seen God work subtly in the past?
3. What areas in your own life do you need to see with the eyes of faith and be reminded of God's subtle and inconspicuous providence?

CHAPTER THREE

# A CINDERELLA STORY (ONLY SEEDIER) (2:1–18)

*[God] does not throw down men at random on the earth, to go wherever they please, but guides all by his secret purpose. (John Calvin[1])*

In many ways, Esther's rise to power in the Persian Empire resembles the story of Cinderella. In the fairy tale, the prince is in search of his true love, so he gathers all the eligible bachelorettes in the kingdom to a ball. When Cinderella captures his heart, she goes from rags to riches. Similarly, the Persian king Ahasuerus is searching for a new queen, and he also gathers all the eligible bachelorettes in the empire to the royal palace. Esther impresses the king more than anyone else, and she too goes from rags to royal riches. The big difference, however, is that Cinderella captures the royal heart by dancing, whereas Esther has to do more than just dance.

## THE GATHERING OF VIRGINS (2:1–11)

The events leading up to Esther's rise to royal riches begin not long after Vashti's deposition. Ahasuerus's anger has subsided, and now that he has cooled down a bit, he begins to reflect on what has taken place. "He remembered Vashti and what she had done and what had been decreed against her" (2:1). The word translated "remember" means much more than simply recalling to mind the pertinent information; it has a more robust sense to it, having the connotation of recalling something with affection, almost like nostalgia. In other words, Ahasuerus is not simply reviewing dispassionately the events that have transpired; he remembers Vashti warmly and is stricken with regret over the way he treated her. Perhaps he is sorry for his initial summons. Perhaps he is sorry that she complicated the matter by not coming when summoned. Perhaps he is sorry that he acted so rashly. Or perhaps he realizes what he has lost, now that she is gone, and he misses her. Whatever the reasons for his regret, however, there is nothing he can do about it now. He acted impetuously, and now she is irretrievably gone.

Presumably out of concern for the king's unhappiness, some young court attendants come to Ahasuerus with a plan to remedy the situation. Once again, the king is incapable of devising his own plan; his servants must supply it to him. Their proposal is that a search be made over the entire empire, and that all the beautiful young virgins be sent by the commissioners in the provinces to the royal palace, where they can be placed in the king's harem. There, one of the king's top eunuchs will take charge of them, putting them through a strict regimen of beauty treatments. Whichever girl proves most pleasing to the king will become the new queen in Vashti's place. The plan pleases the king, which is not surprising; so far in the book of Esther, extravagant plans that feed into the king's self-indulgence have unfailingly appealed to him.

Characteristically as well, the king seems to have a penchant for plans that are superficial and shortsighted. Unlike virtually every other Persian king, when searching for a wife, Ahasuerus is completely unconcerned about a girl's political or familial significance. Nor are there any criteria pertaining to a girl's character, intelligence, or inner beauty. As far as the king is concerned, there are only three criteria that matter: youth, virginity, and physical beauty. So any girl meeting those three criteria will be gathered into the royal harem, from which he can then choose his next queen.

One of the girls selected is a young Jewish girl named Esther, who is living in Susa.[2] Her father and mother are deceased, and she is being raised by her older cousin, Mordecai, who treats her as if she were his own daughter. Adding to her misfortune is her people's plight. The narrator highlights Mordecai's genealogy and specifically notes the role of the exile in their history.[3] In fact, the verb *carried away* (literally, "exiled") is used three times in the same verse, and the root (*glh*) is used four times, as if to emphasize just how traumatic the ordeal of the exile was. Clearly, Esther is part of a beleaguered people, desperately needing to catch a break. And a break they are about to catch because, in terms of physical appearance, Esther is extremely attractive. She "had a beautiful figure and was lovely to look at" (v. 7), to be exact. Not surprisingly, she was selected and taken into the king's palace.

It is reasonable to suppose that different girls in the empire would have reacted differently to being gathered to Susa for the king's harem. It is not hard to imagine that some girls would have gone against their will, much preferring to stay back in their hometowns with their families and friends. No doubt these girls would have considered life in the harem to have stripped them of their opportunity to marry, have a family, and live among people they loved. However, many of the girls would have been energized with excitement over the privilege of being selected for the king's harem. To those in a modern Western society, that may sound strange. But life was not easy in the ancient world; most people lived a very hard existence. In contrast, life in the king's harem meant living in the lap of luxury. It was a life of ease and privilege. As a result, some young girls would have viewed such a prospect as essentially winning the lottery—a free pass to the good life.

How Esther felt about being selected for the king's harem is left unstated. Some have argued that since the other girls were "gathered," while Esther was "taken," she must have gone against her will.[4] However, the same verb is used in verse 15 to describe Mordecai's adoption of Esther, which can hardly be intended to mean that Mordecai took care of Esther against her will. A more compelling suggestion is that she may have been internally conflicted about her selection. The author identifies her both with her Jewish name, Hadassah, and with a pagan name, Esther. Interestingly, she is the only character in the book who is identified by two different names. The implication is that Esther is caught between two worlds. Part of her identity is rooted in her Jewish heritage; part of her identity is tied up in her Persian culture. As the events of the book unfold, the tension between her two identities will force her to decide between them on several occasions, the first one being almost immediately after she arrives in the royal palace.[5] On the one hand, being true to her Jewish roots would certainly mean avoiding at all costs becoming a pagan king's concubine. On the other hand, living in the cultural climate of the Persians would mean seeing the luxury of the Persian court as something desirable. Esther, it seems, is really caught between two worlds.

Throughout history, people of faith have always found themselves living in the same tension, struggling with whether to be faithful to their core identity among the people of God or whether to capitulate to the pressures of cultural expectations and opportunities. Teenagers regularly find themselves in situations that force them to ask, "Who am I? Am I a follower of Christ—a disciple of Jesus—or am I just part of the crowd? Will I adopt biblical standards on sexuality, or will I adopt the messages of the culture around me? Will I be ethical in my schoolwork, or will I do what everyone else is doing in order to keep pace? Will I boldly live for God no matter what it costs me, or will I hide my faith in embarrassment?" Those in business find themselves in similar challenges. "Am I a Christian who serves in the workplace, or am I a businessman who happens to have some religious commitments on the weekends? Will I adopt the values of corporate America, in which people are treated like commodities and the only thing that matters is the bottom line, or will I adopt the values of Jesus and see inherent value in each person I encounter, whether it is my boss, my subordinate, my colleague, or my customer? Will I operate with such maxims as 'It's not personal; it's business,' and 'All's fair in love and war,' or will I operate out of my Christian identity, seeking to love others as I love myself and to treat them the way I would want to be treated, even when it might mean a disadvantage for me in the competitive marketplace or a lower profit margin?" In fact, every Christian, like Esther, finds himself or herself in situations where one must choose between doing what is right and doing what is culturally acceptable, between acting with integrity and compromising in order to seize an opportunity, between living consistently out of one's identity in Christ and living for whatever is desirable according to the surrounding cultural climate.

## ESTHER'S PREPARATIONS (2:9–13)

In Esther's case, she makes the most of her opportunity by getting close to the eunuch in charge. In fact, the text says that she "gained his favor" or "won his favor." That is different from saying that she found favor. If she had merely "found favor," she would have happened to appeal to the eunuch without much effort on her part. This idiom is different. It is not passive; it is active. Esther seems to have asserted herself in an effort to charm him and gain his favor, eager to make the most of her opportunity.

Apparently, Esther is not only beautiful, but socially shrewd and charming as well.

And her efforts pay off. The eunuch is in charge of preparing each girl in the harem for her one-night audition with the king. In yet another display of royal ostentation in the book, each girl is provided with a twelve-month beauty treatment, consisting of six months with oil of myrrh and six months with perfumes and cosmetics. Actually, the text says that they spend their time in the oil and in the cosmetics, suggesting that these are some sort of fumigation bath treatments that presumably change skin tone and remove spots or blemishes over time.[6] Additionally, each girl is given special food for her diet. For Esther, because she has won the eunuch's favor, he assigns seven of the top maids in the court to her, and she quickly moves to the best place in the harem.

Through all this, Esther is scrupulous to conceal her Jewish identity, presumably by adopting Persian dress, practices, and customs. It isn't entirely clear why she needs to do so; anti-Jewish feelings do not seem to be a widespread problem (Esth. 3:15; 8:15). But by noting this fact, the narrator seems to be indicating which identity she is adopting, and it is not her Jewish one. She clearly does not want to squander this opportunity, and she apparently has no problem hiding her roots to do it. Meanwhile, Mordecai is pacing outside the front of the court of the harem each day in order to remain abreast of Esther's fortunes inside the harem.

After the twelve months of beautification, when it is a girl's turn to spend the night with the king, she is given whatever she wants. She may request anything—clothes, jewelry, perfumes, or anything else. In the evening, she goes into the king's bedroom and "makes her case." Then, in the morning, she comes out and is taken to another harem, this one for the king's concubines, where she lives out a largely plush but pointless existence unless she is fetched once again. Night after night, these bedroom auditions are to continue until the king finds the one he wants to be the new queen.

## THE AMOROUS AUDITION (2:14–18)

Eventually it is Esther's turn, and, according to the date given in verse 16, it has now been four years since Vashti's removal. On the assumption that Ahasuerus did not tarry too long after Vashti's deposition to begin his search, more than one thousand girls may have passed through Ahasuerus's bedroom before it was Esther's turn to audition.[7] Before she enters, she receives some advice from Hegai, the head eunuch, who apparently knows the king's preferences. Acting upon his suggestions, she takes only what he advises her. Unlike the previous queen, who was unwilling to become the king's sexual object, Esther seems only too willing. Then the bedroom door closes.

In the morning, Esther emerges once again, and the king is extremely pleased with her—much more so than with the thousand other girls before her. In fact, the text seems to pile up superlatives describing how delighted the king is with Esther. He loves her more than all the women. She wins grace and favor in his sight more than all the virgins. She is so pleasing that he sets the royal crown on her head—he needs to audition no one else—and gives a great feast for all his officials and servants. In fact, he is so happy that he grants a remission of taxes to the provinces and gives gifts with royal generosity.

Clearly the king is more than just a little pleased with Esther. Subsequent readers, however, have not been nearly so approving. In the postexilic period, maintaining Jewish identity was absolutely critical, and that was achieved primarily through identity markers, such as Sabbath keeping, circumcision, and food laws, as well as injunctions against intermarriage (see Neh. 13, for example). But Esther seems to ignore them all without compunction. Given that she has been trying to conceal her Jewish identity, it is a safe assumption that she has been eating nonkosher food in the Persian court, probably does not observe the Sabbath faithfully, and is more than a little willing to have sex with a pagan, uncircumcised king—hardly the appropriate behavior for a Jewish heroine.

Numerous arguments have been advanced to alleviate the discomfort, all of which try to avoid the association of immoral behavior with the heroine of the story. One tactic has been to argue that Esther never really did anything immoral after all. Additions to the story of Esther try to emphasize her piety; this can be seen both in the Greek version of Esther and in various midrashic treatments of it. In the Septuagint (the Greek translation of the book in the second or first century B.C.), for example, Esther announces her hatred for the bed of the uncircumcised and maintains that she has not eaten nonkosher food or drunk the king's wine.[8] In one midrashic account, Esther tries to hide for four years before she is finally discovered and forcibly taken to the king. In the Babylonian midrashic treatment of Esther, it is argued that Esther was not adopted by Mordecai, but instead was married to him, meaning that she did not actually commit fornication with Ahasuerus. The charge of adultery is then removed by pointing out that she was under duress, making her night with the king akin to rape. In fact, one medieval rabbinic treatment even argues that God actually hid Esther from the king and sent a spirit in her place, so that she never actually had sexual relations with him.[9]

Another tactic has been to concede that Esther did in fact have sex with the pagan king, but to diminish the offensiveness of the act somehow. For instance, some have tried to exonerate Esther by arguing that the passive voice is used for all the verbs, suggesting that Esther was being swept along by circumstances beyond her control. Similarly, some have argued that the Persian court was so powerful that it is unreasonable to expect a young Jewish girl to have been able to stand up to it. However, as Iain Duguid has written, "If someone is willing to suffer the consequences, full obedience to God's law is always an option."[10] After all, Daniel refused the delicacies of the pagan court, no matter what the cost. He was willing to be thrown into a lion's den rather than cease praying. His three friends were willing to be thrown into a blazing furnace rather than give in to the idolatrous demands of a pagan king. Much earlier, Joseph resisted the sexual advances of someone in power and spent years in a dungeon rather than defile himself. And in the postexilic period, Ezra went to great lengths to show the people how wrong intermarriage was and how it was to be avoided at any and all costs.

Finally, a third approach has been to argue that the exigencies of the situation necessitated her actions. For instance, the eleventh-century medieval commentator, Rashi, argued that the righteous Esther's decision to sleep with an uncircumcised Gentile was justifiable because she would eventually rise up to save Israel.[11] Of course, the reader can see that result in hindsight, but it would have been impossible for Esther to know that when she went into the king's bedroom.

The truth is that, at the end of the day, it is very difficult to avoid the most obvious reading of the text, however morally disappointing it is. Esther was a Jewish girl who probably did not follow the dietary laws or observe the Sabbath, and who certainly fornicated with a pagan king. The simple fact is that when she found herself in a hard place, she did not resist. She compromised.

Perhaps, however, the trouble is not so much with the Bible as with our expectations of it. Scripture is not a chronicle of great moral examples, ethical heroes, or spiritual giants. Instead, it is the unfolding story of humanity's brokenness, one sinner at a time, and God's redemptive grace in the midst of it. Abraham lied and doubted, but God worked his providential grace through him. Moses became impatient, but God still worked through him.

David committed adultery and murder, but God still worked through him. Throughout Scripture, God's people morally compromise, ethically fail, and persistently sin; yet, amazingly, God providentially and graciously continues to use them for his redemptive purposes. And the same thing is true for Esther. She is culpable for her failures. Her compromises cannot be excused, downplayed, or explained away. Yet, in the larger context of the book, this young girl's moral compromises are used by God to deliver his people from potential extermination.

## MORAL COMPROMISE AND GOD'S SOVEREIGN GRACE

Many years later, God would do the very same thing in what would prove to be one of the worst moral compromises imaginable (John 18:1–27). After praying in Gethsemane, Jesus was arrested by a band of soldiers and officers sent from the chief priests and the Pharisees. Jesus was then bound and brought to Annas, and then to the house of the high priest, Caiaphas. While Jesus was inside, Peter, who had followed behind them at a distance, stood outside in the courtyard. Inside, false witnesses were paraded before the high priest to offer false testimony against Jesus in what was nothing more than a kangaroo court. But those were not the worst lies that were told, nor were they the worst betrayals, for outside Peter began to be questioned too. One of the servant girls of the high priest saw Peter and said, "You also are not one of this man's disciples, are you?" But Peter denied it, saying, "I am not." Then he went over by a fire and began warming himself. As he was standing there, some of the bystanders asked him, "You also are not one of his disciples, are you?" Again, Peter denied it and said, "I am not." Then another servant of the high priest recognized him and said, "Did I not see you in the garden with him?" And for a third time, Peter denied it.

Immediately a rooster crowed, just as Jesus had predicted. Peter, suddenly aware of what he had done, broke down and wept (Mark 14:72).

One can only imagine the guilt, sorrow, and regret that Peter felt at that moment. Knowing that he had just denied Jesus, the Son of God and his Lord, at that critical moment, must have been almost too much to bear. Jesus was being tried on trumped-up charges and would be brutally beaten and crucified, and Peter, through his inexcusable moral compromise, denied him and left him twisting in the wind.

Nevertheless, Jesus would not leave Peter. In fact, even as Peter was denying him as he went to the cross, Jesus' concern was to redeem Peter and everyone like him. His mission was to die and rise again for the redemption of moral compromisers like Peter and like us. And so, after rising from the dead and appearing to the disciples on the shore of the Sea of Galilee, Jesus asked Peter three times if he loved him (John 21:15–19). Each time Peter answered in the affirmative, and each time Jesus gave him a commission to tend (or feed) his sheep. Three times Peter had denied him; three times Jesus gave him a significant pastoral role for the people of God. Despite Peter's terrible moral compromise, God redeemed him and transformed his craven denials into pastoral commissions. Through it all, Peter came to understand that even as he was betraying Jesus, Jesus was redeeming him and using him for his greater purposes.

What good news this is for us to hear today. How many times, like Esther, have we been willing to compromise because we were unwilling to suffer the consequences for doing what was right? How many times have we rationalized it by telling ourselves that we really didn't have a choice? How many times have we chosen to conform to the cultural standard rather than to live out our core identity as someone whom Christ has redeemed and made new? Some, like Esther, have compromised in the area of sexual morality, having engaged in premarital or extramarital sex. Some, like Esther, have married or are considering marrying someone who does not share their faith. Some, like Esther, have preferred to chase opportunity no matter what the cost, sacrificing family, integrity, or friendships to get ahead. Still others, like Esther, have tried to hide who they really are, concealing their identity as someone who belongs to God, unwilling to live unashamedly as a Christian, or even denying it in order to fit in.

Yet the glorious news of the gospel is that God is able to gather up our moral failures and still use them for something redemptive and glorious in the end. The cross itself says so. It tells us that there is nothing that is unredeemable. God is able to take our failures and incorporate them into his larger redemptive purposes. That doesn't make what we've done right, and it doesn't mean that there aren't high prices to pay for what we've done, and it certainly doesn't mean—as Paul's opponents suggested—that we should sin all the more, so that grace may abound. The answer to that is, and always has been, heaven forbid! But it also doesn't mean that our failures are unredeemable. In the words of a Portuguese proverb, "God writes straight, but with crooked lines."[12] The remarkable, even scandalous, truth is that God's providence is strong enough and his grace is big enough to take the crooked lines of our moral compromises and to "write straight" his larger redemptive story. Thus, there is hope for us, just as there was for Esther.

There is hope for the one who has been sexually immoral. For the single man or woman who has allowed a relationship to progress too far physically, there can sometimes be overwhelming guilt and regret. Some may wonder if the innocence they have lost will forever mar them and haunt them. They may wonder whether they have spoiled their current relationship beyond repair. They may wonder whether a future husband or wife will be able to overlook their past or forgive what they've done. Or they may wonder whether God can still use them. This can be an especially burdensome worry if a single night, one foolish indiscretion, has left them with permanent consequences, such as an incurable disease or an unwanted pregnancy. Yet God's sovereign grace is bigger than one night, no matter how foolish. God's grace is bigger than any compromises we've made. Even the biggest mistakes can be redeemed for his purposes. Perhaps the unwanted pregnancy becomes a gift that transforms a young woman's life. Perhaps that child will be used for great things in God's plan. Perhaps a disease can be used by God to refocus a person's attention on the things that really matter and to help guard him from further self-destructive behaviors that would otherwise be all too easy for him to fall into. Perhaps God will use the guilt and regret to open up a young woman to a deeper appreciation of his grace in Christ than would have otherwise been possible for her to grasp. Like the prostitute in Luke's gospel who shamelessly comes into a Pharisee's house and begins to wipe Jesus' feet with her tears and hair and to anoint him with ointment, perhaps God will use a young woman's sexual immorality to teach her to love much because she has been forgiven much (Luke 7:36–50). Only God knows for sure. However, Esther shows us beyond the shadow of a doubt that God's sovereign grace can use even sexual immorality, whether premarital or extramarital, in a redemptive way to accomplish his sovereign purposes.

Likewise, there is also hope for the Christian who has married a non-Christian husband or wife, all the while knowing it is wrong. For the Christian married to a non-Christian, it is easy to become overwhelmed with feelings of regret, of being trapped, and of hopelessness. Marriage can be challenging enough when two people share the same values and worship the same God. But when a husband and a wife have differing ultimate values and have hearts that are committed to different things, it can make those same challenges even more difficult and can introduce many new ones as well. A Christian in such a marriage can find himself feeling locked into a very painful and frustrating situation without any biblical grounds for changing it. As a result, the regret and despair can seem debilitating. Yet God's sovereign grace is bigger than a marriage wrongly entered. Perhaps God will use the marriage to lead the unbelieving spouse to faith in Christ. As Peter writes to wives in just this situation,

> Likewise, wives, be subject to your own husbands, so that even if some do not obey the word, they may be won without a word by the conduct of their wives—when they see your respectful and pure conduct. (1 Peter 3:1–2)

However, even if the unbelieving spouse never comes to faith, God may still use the relationship to refine the faith and perseverance of the believing spouse. Moreover, as Paul suggests, even if the unbelieving spouse never comes to faith, God still uses the believing spouse in a sanctifying way for the rest of the family. He writes,

> If any woman has a husband who is an unbeliever, and he consents to live with her, she should not divorce him. For the unbelieving husband is made holy because of his wife, and the unbelieving wife is made holy because of her husband. Otherwise your children would be unclean, but as it is, they are holy. (1 Cor. 7:13–14)

The ideal, of course, is for Christians to marry Christians (2 Cor. 6:14); however, even when Christians compromise and marry non-Christians, as was the case with Esther, God's sovereign grace can still redeem the relationship for his sovereign purposes.

Finally, there is hope as well for the one who has pursued a career for all the wrong reasons. People of faith should ideally pursue work that has a sense of calling for them. God has endowed each person with a unique set of gifts, and he gives each of us a responsibility to enter our work as a service to him with those gifts (Col. 3:23). However, it is all too common for someone to choose a line of work for entirely different reasons, such as expediency, money, ambition, or prestige. A high school friend of mine decided to attend a particular college and major in a particular field solely because of what the average starting salary for that line of work was. Such reasons, as they did for my friend, almost always lead to regret, frustration, and unhappiness. Many fail to wake up to that reality until they have the proverbial midlife crisis. Suddenly, they realize they may have been pursuing all the wrong things for decades. However, God is able to redeem even our most misguided steps. Our motives may have been full of crooked lines, but God can still "write straight" with them. Though we may have chosen a career for unwise reasons, perhaps God desires to use us where we are. Perhaps we have a role to play in that industry or in the culture of that company. Perhaps God will use us in the lives of those in the cubicles around us and will make something of our misguided decision that landed us there in the first place. Perhaps we have ended up in a position solely because of our opportunistic scheming, just like Esther, and yet God may end up using our sin for his larger purposes. Who knows? That is the wonder of God's sovereign grace. He can redeem the seemingly unredeemable. He can "write straight" with very crooked lines.

Gordon Macdonald tells a story set in southern England along the sea.[13] One evening in an English pub filled with drinkers, there was a storm raging outside. As the storm grew worse, more and more people came in to get out of the elements. As people were eating and drinking, they were bumping into one another as they made their way through the crowd, laughing and gesturing. At one point, a waitress came through the crowd with a tray, holding it high with cups of ale, coffee, and tea. As she was making her way through the pub, someone accidentally jostled her and the ale, coffee, and tea went flying and splashed all over a recently painted wall.

The proprietor of the pub was very angry that his newly painted wall was now ruined. The whole crowd fell silent as they waited to see what he would do. The humiliated waitress stood frozen, when suddenly from the corner of the pub a man spoke out, saying, "If you will permit me, perhaps I can do something about that." Stepping forward, he opened up a little case, filled with an artist's brushes and paints, which he was carrying with him. The crowd stood aside and the man began to work intently on the wall that was now so stained. He began to sketch with his charcoal and then with his paint.

The crowd watched as he went about his work, and after forty-five minutes or so, there before them was a beautiful painting. The stains had been turned into something that was absolutely breathtaking. When the man was through, he stepped back, and it was almost as if everyone in the pub gasped together at the beauty of what was now before them. Then the artist took a piece of charcoal and signed his name in the lower left-hand corner, quickly wrapped up the tools of his artistry, and went out the door, disappearing into the storm. When the people leaned in to look at the name, they discovered that they had been watching one of England's greatest artists at work, and they had seen him take something that was ugly and turn it into something that was beautiful.

Such is the powerful and sovereign grace of God. Whatever compromises you have made, whatever failures you have had, the truth of the matter is that God is subtly at work even in the midst of them. His providence is stronger than your compromises; his grace is greater than your failures. Like the artist in the pub, he is a God who takes the very blemishes and blotches of our lives and uses them, redeems them, and transforms them, by his grace, into something beautiful.

## FOR FURTHER REFLECTION

1. Where have you been tempted to compromise your morals in order to get ahead in the world?
2. In what situations are you tempted to privatize your faith or conceal your identity as a Christian?
3. What moral failures are you tempted to think God cannot redeem and cannot use in his larger purposes?
4. How can the grace of God in the cross of Christ empower you to live faithfully in the world, no matter what the cost?

CHAPTER FOUR

# HELL HATH NO FURY LIKE AN AGAGITE SCORNED (2:19–3:15)

*God is to be trusted when his providences seem to run contrary to his promises. (Thomas Watson[1])*

A temporal gap exists between Esther 2:18 and 2:19. Some amount of time has elapsed since Esther's rise to the throne, though it is left unstated exactly how much time has passed. However, if the events of 2:19–23 are near in time to the events of 3:1–15, then approximately five years have elapsed (3:7). In the meantime, an empire united in the celebration of a new queen has given way to a period of internal dissension inside the royal acropolis itself.

## MORDECAI DISCOVERS A PLOT (2:19–23)

At some point, another gathering of virgins at the royal place is commissioned. The narrator does not explain why there would be a second gathering, though several explanations have been suggested.[2] One suggestion is that this was a second wave of virgins who had come from great distances away, but arrived only after Esther had been chosen. Another suggestion is that the courtiers became envious of Esther's influence on the king and so tried to find a replacement. Others have proposed that the statement is a parenthetical remark that refers to the time of Esther's gathering. On this view, there was a first gathering that did not include Esther and a second gathering narrated in 2:1–4. Still others have suggested that the second gathering refers not to a new batch of women, but to a second gathering of the same women gathered in 2:1–4. On this reading, the first gathering brought these young women to the royal palace, while the second gathering moved them to the harem. Finally, there is the possibility that even after a queen was chosen, the king continued to gather young women for his pleasure. Since it has the fewest difficulties, the last suggestion is probably the correct one.

As it turns out, Mordecai was "sitting at the king's gate" while this was happening. This does not mean that Mordecai was loitering at the entrance to the palace. The king's gate would have been a large building at the entrance of the palace complex where legal matters and commercial transactions were handled.[3] Thus, "sitting at the king's gate" was an idiom that meant to hold office in the palace administration.[4] An analogous modern-day example would be the phrase "sitting on the bench" when used for a judge. To say that a judge is sitting on the bench does not mean that he is sitting on a long wooden seat; it means that he is presiding in a court of law. Similarly, to say that Mordecai was "sitting at the king's gate" means that he was holding some kind of office within the palace administration when this second gathering took place. Whether he had held his post for some time or whether he was newly appointed through the nepotistic influence of Esther is not revealed, even if it proves to be especially fortuitous.

During this time, for reasons left unstated, two of the king's eunuchs, Bigthan and Teresh, become angry at the king and devise a plan to assassinate him ("lay hands on him"). Their plan should be easy to carry out because their role is to guard the threshold, which means that they have times of easy access to the king.

Somehow or another, Mordecai gets wind of their plan and tells Esther what he has discovered. Esther then relays it to the king, making sure that the king knows that it was Mordecai who uncovered the murderous plot. An investigation is launched, the facts are confirmed, and the two conspiring eunuchs are executed on the gallows. Mordecai's name and his good deed are then recorded in the king's record book—a detail that will prove crucial as the story unfolds.

## MORDECAI SPURNS HAMAN (3:1–4)

Having just been told of Mordecai's heroic rescue of the king, the reader would normally expect to read at the beginning of chapter 3 that the king rewards Mordecai. After all, the king now owes his life to him, and Persian kings are known to be especially careful to reward such acts.[5] Perhaps the king might compensate him with a monetary reward or tax exemption, or honor him with a public ceremony, or bestow upon him a well-deserved promotion within the administrative ranks of the empire. And, in fact, a man is promoted—but not Mordecai! Instead, a man named Haman is promoted—and King Ahasuerus even makes him the second most powerful man in the empire. Moreover, the king commands all his servants to bow down and pay homage to Haman.

As will become clear, this is much worse than mere negligence for Mordecai. Haman is introduced as Haman the Agagite, meaning that he is a descendant of Agag the Amalekite. When Israel came out of Egypt, the Amalekites attacked them in the wilderness and tried to destroy them (Ex. 17:8–16). As a result, God cursed the Amalekites and ordered that their memory be blotted out from the face of the earth (Deut. 25:17–19; cf. Num. 24:7). Later, when Saul became Israel's first king, he was ordered to carry out the sentence on the Amalekites and on King Agag in particular. However, he disobeyed the Lord and spared Agag (1 Sam. 15:1–9). Ever after, there was bitter rivalry and antagonism between the Amalekites and the Israelites. Consequently, the promotion of Haman the Agagite to the second most powerful position in the empire strikes an ominous chord.

The ancestry of Mordecai makes it even more foreboding. In Esther 2:5–6, Mordecai was introduced as the son of Jair, son of Shimei, son of Kish, a Benjaminite. In other words, Mordecai is a descendant of King Saul.[6] One can easily imagine how bitter it would have been for this descendant of Saul to see not only his own good deed go unrewarded, but also a descendant of Agag elevated to the highest possible position next to the king himself.

Not surprisingly, Mordecai simply cannot bring himself to bow down before an Agagite such as Haman or to pay homage to him. Not that Haman notices; he apparently is too absorbed in soaking up the adulation of the crowd to notice that Mordecai is standing, not bowing. However, the other officials notice, and they ask him why he refuses to comply with the king's command to bow down to Haman. The question could either be a rhetorical one, meant to rebuke Mordecai, or be a genuine inquiry, seeking to understand why Mordecai is being insubordinate. Either way, Mordecai does not answer. Not content, they continue to ask him day after day. But, again and again, Mordecai does not listen to them.

Mordecai's silence has been interpreted in various ways. Some have taken it to mean that Mordecai has grown tired of their incessant questioning and simply refuses to listen to them any longer. Others have suggested that Mordecai is revealing his recalcitrant stubbornness and thus simply refuses to explain himself. However, a third and more compelling option is possible. Mordecai's silence could be part of his characterization as a man of wisdom.[7]

He has already been portrayed as gracious in raising his younger cousin, Esther, after her parents died, as wise in his directions to her when she was brought into the palace, and as shrewd in reporting the conspiracy, not directly to the king or through other officials, who may or may not have been in league with the conspirators, but indirectly through Esther. Now he finds himself unable to bow down before Haman as a matter of conscience but, in his wisdom, he wishes to remain quiet about it in order not to stir up trouble. The last thing he wants is to make the long-standing enmity between the Agagites and the Israelites an issue within the palace courts. That could only inflame the situation and lead to more trouble.

So he resolves to keep quiet. But at some point he divulges to them that he is a Jew, hoping that will be enough to satisfy them. The officials, however, want to check out the validity of Mordecai's reason, and so they report the matter directly to Haman, to see whether he will let the matter stand (a somewhat humorous way to put it, since the issue is whether Mordecai himself will stand or bow) or whether he will press for Mordecai's compliance.

The irony is twofold. First, the report to Haman puts Mordecai in a position opposite to the one he previously enjoyed. When Mordecai found out that two officials had turned on the king, he informed him of the betrayal. Now, other officials find out that Mordecai has turned on the king's right-hand man, and they inform him of Mordecai's betrayal. Second, the report accomplishes exactly what Mordecai was trying to avoid. By keeping silent, Mordecai was attempting to keep the peace as much as possible. However, with the officials' report to Haman, the peace is broken.

## HAMAN PLOTS AGAINST THE JEWS (3:5–15)

The peace is broken, of course, because the hatred is mutual. When Haman is informed that Mordecai refuses to bow down before him, his pride is wounded and he becomes enraged. In fact, his rage is so intense that he decides to destroy not just Mordecai, but all his fellow Jews as well. This extreme reaction can only mean that the age-old hatred for the Jews has now been brought to the surface by Mordecai's action. Haman's response is not just against Mordecai, but against what Mordecai represents, namely, the long-standing enmity between Israelites and Amalekites. As a result, all the Jews throughout the Persian Empire also become the objects of Haman's hatred.

Haman gathers the diviners together to determine the best day, according to the gods, for him to carry out his diabolical plan to destroy all the Jews within the empire. They do this by casting lots, which may be something like modern-day dice,[8] for each day on the calendar in succession until the most propitious day is determined by how the lots fall. As they move through the calendar, it is eventually the twelfth month for which the lots give the sought-after date.

With his plan now devised, Haman goes to the king to secure his support. Shrewdly, he begins with a truth: "There is a certain people scattered abroad and dispersed among the peoples." Then he moves on to a half-truth: "Their laws are different." He finishes with an outright lie: "They do not keep the king's laws."[9] In short, Haman is suggesting that these people are different, difficult, and dangerous. If something is not done about them, he implies, they will at the very least cause disorder within the empire and, quite possibly, pose an imminent and widespread threat to king and empire.[10] Consequently, Haman implores, they should be dealt with, and it would be in the king's best interest to issue a decree to that end. Then Haman sweetens the deal by offering to put 10,000 talents (more than 300 tons) of silver in the royal treasury. Unless this is just rhetorical flourish or hyperbole, such a sum is completely unreasonable; ten thousand talents is roughly two-thirds of the empire's annual revenue! Nonetheless,

Haman is so consumed with rage that he is willing to make an outlandish pledge to try to secure the king's support.

The king, as is typical by now, isn't thinking straight. Actually, he isn't thinking much at all. The proposal would take away a portion of his tax base, but that never seems to occur to him.[11] The bribe that Haman promises is something he will never be able to deliver, but the king apparently does not realize that. Nor does it even occur to the king that a bribe would be unnecessary if the proposed plan really were in the king's best interest, as Haman pretends. No supporting evidence for the accusations is produced, but the king never thinks to require it. Nor does he call in his royal advisers to seek their counsel before making his decision. Instead, in his suddenly incited paranoia over a possible mutiny, he simply hands over his signet ring, effectively giving Haman a blank check to do whatever he wants to do to this unnamed but apparently seditious people. In doing so, he unwittingly abets a plan to destroy the very man who has just uncovered a plot to destroy him![12]

Once again, the royal mail service is used to punish the people in the empire who are in solidarity with someone who is refusing to obey the king's command. The royal scribes are summoned, and an edict is drafted to be sent out to the king's satraps and to the governors over all the provinces and to the officials of all the peoples. In fact, the verbs used to describe the whole process—"were summoned," "was written," "was sealed," "were sent," "was to be issued," "to be ready"—are all in the passive voice, which conveys "an impression of the cold, relentless, and impersonal nature of the process."[13]

Yet, as cold and heartless as the process itself is, the content of the edict is far more so. Written in the native language of each of the peoples within the empire, the edict instructs everyone in the empire (not the imperial army!) to destroy, kill, and annihilate all Jews, young and old, women and children, in one day. Obviously, the language evidences both hatred and totality. The piling up of verbs—destroy, kill, annihilate—when one would have been sufficient, reveals the all-consuming hatred of the Jews that Haman feels. The terms themselves, along with the provision for looting, are taken from military law during wartime and reveal the kind of brutal force he wishes to use against them.[14] Clearly, he leaves no doubt about what he wants done to them and what kind of force he wants used. And neither does he leave doubt about who should be destroyed, killed, and annihilated. The edict does not stop with "all Jews." Certainly, that would cover them all, but Haman wants to make clear that they are to kill every Jew from the youngest to the oldest and not just the men either, but the women and children as well.

The edict also informs the peoples of the date that has been set for this annihilation, the thirteenth day of the twelfth month. That, of course, raises the question as to why the edict would be sent out so early. Why not wait until closer to the twelfth month? The reason cannot be administrative; the Persian administrative system was highly efficient. Nor can the reason be logistical; the necessary preparations could not have required nearly a year to make. Presumably, the only conceivable reason is that Haman wants to prolong the agony of the Jews. There is nowhere for them to escape within the Persian Empire. All they can do is wait in agony for eleven months, with their executions approaching closer and closer by the day.

No doubt the agony would have been intensified for many Jews when they realized that the edict was issued on the day before Passover. The sense of reversal would have been both ironic and bitter. Since Passover was an annual festival celebrating their forefathers' deliverance from the oppression of Pharaoh, the edict's timing would have been a bitter pill to swallow, since it was decreeing their destruction under the oppression of Haman. But it would have been painfully ironic as well. The selection of the Passover lamb would have taken place on the tenth of Nisan; similarly, the selection of the Jews for slaughter by Haman also took place on the tenth of Nisan. The correlation is impossible to miss.[15] In Egypt, their forefathers would have slaughtered the Passover lambs as a means for their escape; now the edict indicates that the Jews themselves will be slaughtered, and there is no hope of escape.

Moreover, the edict seeks to drum up anti-Jewish sentiments among the people by promising the other peoples of the empire the opportunity to plunder the Jews' property after their executions. For many people, the prospect of material gain would have been enough of a reason to support the genocide and wait for it with anticipation.

Thus, the couriers go out hurriedly by order of the king, and the edict is issued within the capital city of Susa, while copies of the edict are delivered throughout the empire and proclaimed to all the people. Within the city of Susa, confusion erupts, presumably because the people cannot imagine what would prompt such a brutal extermination. In contrast, the scene within the palace is a calm but chilling one. Callously, the king and Haman sit down to drink.

## ATTACKS AGAINST GOD'S PEOPLE AND THE GRACIOUS PROVIDENCE OF GOD

Within the flow of history, Haman's heartless plan to destroy all the Jews within the empire on account of his rival Mordecai is a distressing adumbration of another attack, for similar reasons, many years later. In the gospel of Matthew, wise men from the east see a star rising in the sky and interpret it to mean that a king of the Jews has been born. Journeying to Jerusalem, they ask where this newborn king is, for they desire to bow down before him and worship. Much like Haman, Herod becomes incensed that a rival might challenge him and devises an insidious and evil plan. He calls the chief priests and the scribes of the people and inquires of them where the Messiah is to be born. Citing a prophecy from Micah, they tell him that the birthplace is to be Bethlehem. He immediately calls for the wise men and requests that they inform him when they locate the child. The wise men, however, are warned in a dream and do not return to Herod with the requested information. As a result, just as Haman was willing to exterminate a whole group of people to get at one person who rivaled him, so Herod is willing to exterminate a whole group of people to get at one person who rivals him. And, like Haman, he sends out a notice for the extermination, this time for all the male children in Bethlehem, and, consequently, like Susa, the surrounding area is thrown into great turmoil (Matt. 2:1–18).

The one big difference, however, is that the male children of Bethlehem, unlike the Jews in the Persian Empire, were not spared. Tragically, they perished. And though Jesus would providentially be spared from Herod's heartless attack, the attacks on him would not stop. The Pharisees attacked him. The Sadducees attacked him. The chief priests, scribes, and elders attacked him, ultimately plotting a way to arrest him and put him to death. And just as Haman was willing to pay silver for the death of Mordecai, so too were these leaders willing to pay silver for the death of Jesus. Convicted on bogus charges, just as the Jews in Persia were, Jesus was condemned at their merciless hands. They beat him, mocked him, and then nailed him to a cross.

But the attacks did not stop with Jesus. Just as Haman's attacks went beyond Mordecai to those in solidarity with him, so the attacks went beyond Jesus to those in solidarity with him as well. Much like the Jews were targeted by the mighty Persian Empire, so early Christians were targeted at times by the mighty Roman Empire, which demanded the same kind of honor from their citizens that Haman demanded. As Karen Jobes describes it,

> The Roman emperors demanded "respect" by issuing a decree that an offering of incense must be burnt in their honor. All good citizens of the empire would in this way express their appreciation for the benefits and well-being the Roman emperor provided. When Christians saw that demand to be in conflict with their allegiance to Jesus Christ and refused to pay such honor, the charge brought against them was treason, a political crime punishable by death.[16]

In the book of Revelation, these attacks are described with vivid apocalyptic imagery that frames the conflict in larger cosmic terms. God's people are portrayed as a sun-clothed woman who gives birth to a male child (Jesus). However, a great red dragon (symbolizing Satan himself) seeks to devour the child as soon as he is born (an allusion to Herod's attack). The child, however, is protected from his attacks. Having failed to devour the child, the dragon then turns his attention to the woman herself, pursuing her as he had pursued the child. When she too is protected, he becomes even more furious and goes off to make war with her offspring (Rev. 12:1–17).

In order to accomplish his evil designs, Satan raises up earthly empires who will persecute God's people, represented by the images of a beast rising up out of the sea and a beast rising up out of the earth (Rev. 13:1–18). These beastly empires will demand worship from those under them. Whoever refuses to do so will be put to death. So terrible, in fact, will the persecutions be that those who have been martyred for their allegiance to God will continually cry out from underneath an altar, "O Sovereign Lord, holy and true, how long before you will judge and avenge our blood on those who dwell on the earth?" (Rev. 6:10).

This is a question that has been asked throughout the centuries. In just the years 54–304, there were ten separate periods of persecution within the Roman Empire, accounting for 193 of the 250 years.[17] And now, in the last hundred years, the number of Christians persecuted and killed for their faith exceeds, by some estimates, the total of the previous nineteen centuries. Much of it is state-sponsored (usually in Communist or Islamic states), but not all of it. Some of it occurs in societies in which the state does little if anything to stop it. As one recent book states,

> Persecution can be government sponsored as a matter of policy or practice, as in North Korea, Vietnam, China, Burma, Saudi Arabia, and Iran. It can be the result of hostility within the society and carried out by extremists and vigilantes who operate with impunity or are beyond the government's ability to control. That is the situation today in Nigeria and Iraq. It can also be carried out by terrorist groups exerting control over territories, such as the Al-Shabab in Somalia and the Taliban in Afghanistan. Or it can come from the hands of combined and conflicting powers, as in Egypt and Pakistan.[18]

Though Christians in modern, Western nations have rarely endured the kinds of attacks experienced by the Jews in the book of Esther, the male children in Bethlehem, the early Christians in the Roman Empire, or modern-day Christians in many Communist or Islamic states, most have suffered in some way from Satan's enmity in this broken world.

Sometimes the suffering can be physical. The rates of physical and sexual abuse continue to increase at alarming rates. Violence continues to escalate within our culture, with more and more people being victimized. Christians are not immune and at times suffer from physical attacks simply because they are Christians.

Sometimes the suffering can be psychological or emotional. Haman wasn't content to destroy the Jews; he wanted to subject them to eleven months of psychological agony too. Similarly, some today endure psychological assaults. In relationships, an ex-spouse knows just how to press the right buttons. In school, a bully terrorizes other classmates simply because he can and it gives him pleasure. Again, Christians endure these kinds of attacks as much as anyone else, and sometimes endure them simply because they are trying to be faithful to Christ. The damage can be significant, and the scars can be lasting.

Perhaps nothing raises the question of where God is and what he is doing more than persecution in particular and suffering more generally. With the souls under the altar in Revelation, we cry out, "O Sovereign Lord, . . . how long?" (Rev. 6:10). We wonder why God would allow it and whether there is any redeemable purpose in it.

And though we may never know why God has allowed any particular suffering or attack, we can at least know that he is not absent in the midst of it. We can know that he is working out his purposes, even if we do not understand how he is doing so or why we are suffering the particular attacks that we are. The cross tells us so. On the cross, God himself stood in the path of the full fury of the world's hatred and violence. He took it upon himself to be *with* us there, and he took it upon himself *for* us. Therefore, even when we are attacked, when we are victimized and are suffering from the evil plots of others, and when we wonder what God is doing in all of it, we may not know or ever know everything he is doing or why he would allow it to happen, but we do know this: he *is* working. His work may be subtle, even inconspicuous, but it can also be redemptive.

Thus, when the attacks come, when others plot evil against us, the cross assures us that God is still working, even if we can't see it. The cross assures us that God is with us, even when we can't feel it. The cross assures us that God's redemptive purposes are greater than the evil being done. As we look in faith to the cross, our hearts are lifted up in the midst of the pain, so that instead of being filled with anger, they can be filled with grace and hope.

Perhaps they can even be filled with a supernatural forgiveness as well. Perhaps, as we look in faith to Christ on the cross, we too can say, "Father, forgive them, for they know not what they do" (Luke 23:34). (Incidentally, Luke tells us that Jesus spoke these words as the soldiers were casting lots!) We can look at those who are attacking us and still detect God's invisible hand at work and can pray for his redemptive purposes to be worked out in their hearts, even as we pray for his purposes to be worked out in our own hearts.

A moving example of this supernatural forgiveness of one's attackers is found in the life and ministry of Hassan Dehqani-Tafti, the Anglican bishop of Iran during the years of the Iranian Revolution. Born to a Muslim father and a Christian mother, Hassan became a Christian during his teenage years. Conscripted, he served in the Iranian army during World War II, before preparing for ordination at Cambridge. Eventually, he became the bishop of Iran and was known for establishing schools and working to help the blind.

However, Dehqani-Tafti endured enormous suffering in the course of his ministry. When Ayatollah Khomeini led the infamous Iranian Revolution in 1979, Bishop Dehqani-Tafti urged a move toward a just, equal, and free society. But the opposite happened. Church hospitals and missions were seized, church property was looted, and pastors were arrested, as Khomeini and his supporters attempted to consolidate power and suppress dissenting voices. Within a few months of the coup, gunmen who were part of a fanatical revolutionary movement broke into Bishop Hassan's house during the night, stormed into his bedroom, and began firing shots. Hassan's wife, Margaret, quickly threw herself across his body. Though the gun was only one foot from Hasan, miraculously the four bullets fired at him ripped through his pillow, leaving a semicircle of holes around his head. A fifth shot went through Margaret's hand. Several months later, Hassan's secretary was shot and wounded. Soon after that, as Hassan's son, Bahram, was returning from work, his car was ambushed, and he was shot and killed.

One can only imagine the emotions that the bishop must have felt after he and his wife had been attacked, his secretary assailed, and his son killed. How could one not be filled with anger, bitterness, and a desire for vengeance? Yet Hassan Dehqani-Tafti could not help but see his own experience through the lens of the cross. Doing so enabled him to experience a deeper sense of solidarity with Christ, who also was attacked. As a result, though grief stricken and pained, he was supernaturally filled with compassion, love, and even forgiveness. As he thought about those who had persecuted him, his loved ones, and his family, particularly his son, he composed the following prayer:

> O God,
> We remember not only Bahram but also his murderers;
> Not because they killed him in the prime of his youth
> and made our hearts bleed and our tears flow;
> Not because with this savage act they have brought
> further disgrace on the name of our country
> among the civilized world;
> But because through their crime we now follow thy
> foot-steps more closely in the way of sacrifice.
> The terrible fire of the calamity burns up all selfish-
> ness and possessiveness in us;
> Its flame reveals the depth of depravity and meanness
> and suspicion, the dimension of hatred and
> the measure of sinfulness in human nature;
> It makes obvious as never before our need to trust
> in God's love as shown in the cross of Jesus
> and his resurrection;
> Love which makes us free from hate towards our
> persecutors;
> Love which brings patience, forbearance, courage, loy-
> alty, humility, generosity, greatness of heart;

Love which more than ever deepens our trust in
God's final victory and his eternal designs
for the Church and for the world;
Love which teaches us how to prepare ourselves to
face our own day of death.
O God,
Bahram's blood has multiplied the fruit of the Spirit
in the soil of our souls;
So when his murderers stand before thee on the day
of judgment
Remember the fruit of the Spirit by which they have
enriched our lives.
And forgive.[19]

In composing such a prayer, Dehqani-Tafti understood that the attacks and persecutions he and his family faced were not meaningless acts of hatred; they were acts that held the potential to conform him to the way of the cross. The persecutions were not just random and pointless; they led him to trust in the grace of God in the death and resurrection of Christ—and, in trusting more deeply, to be filled with that same grace and love toward others, even his persecutors. As such, the attacks upon him and his family became not just moments of pain for Dehqani-Tafti, but moments of grace—moments in which he understood the suffering of Christ on his behalf more deeply, the love of God in Christ more powerfully, and the forgiveness of God through the cross more richly.

Perhaps it is inevitable that when we are attacked or victimized, we should wonder where God is and what he is doing. And even though we will likely never know the full extent of his purposes in our trials, we do know this: even when we are the objects of hatred, even when we are the victims of evil plots and schemes, even when we are attacked, God is still at work. His work may be subtle, and often is, but it is also redemptive. In those very moments of pain, he draws us closer to himself, so close in fact that we just might experience the feel of the wood of the cross, the cold of the nails, and the prick of the thorns. But we will also feel the beating of his heart, the compassion of his eyes, and the warmth of his embrace—so that the attacks against us become not just moments of pain, but also moments of grace.

## FOR FURTHER REFLECTION

1. When have you suffered from an unjust attack because of your ethnicity or faith? How did you respond?
2. Why do personal attacks cause us to question God's character and/or involvement in our lives?
3. How does the cross help us to make some sense of what God is doing by allowing attacks to come against us? How can a crucified Christ reshape our hearts to respond in a different way than we normally would?

CHAPTER FIVE

# THE MOMENT OF TRUTH (4:1–17)

*Providence is God's lantern in many affairs; if we do not follow it close, we may be left in the dark, and lose our way. (Stephen Charnock[1])*

Haman's devilish edict has now been sent to all the provinces of the empire. In eleven months, the Jews will be slaughtered en masse and their goods will be plundered.

## MORDECAI AND THE JEWS MOURN (4:1–3)

For the second time in the book, Mordecai learns of the inner machinations of the royal palace. That he "learned all that had been done" (4:1) means that he knows more than what the edict itself contains; he has come to know what went into it, including, as will become evident, the details of Haman's dirty bribe. Understandably, Mordecai is distraught. As the king and Haman sit down coolly and calmly for a drink, Mordecai becomes frantic. As a sign of his distress, he tears his clothes, puts on sackcloth, and sprinkles ashes on his head. Throughout the Bible, such actions are the typical ways of expressing grief, lamentation, anguish, and distress; they symbolically identify with death itself through a process of dramatization.[2] Consequently, such things are usually done after a calamity, not before it.[3] But not here—the fact that Mordecai begins his acts of ritual mourning before the slaughter is a testament to how irrevocably doomed he and his people are.

Then he begins walking through the city, crying out and weeping bitterly. Of course, as the news spreads throughout the empire, all the other Jews have similar responses. They too begin to mourn, fast, weep, lament, and put on sackcloth and ashes. The contrast is stark. Up to this point, the food, clothing, and cosmetics within the story have been festive and luxuriant. But now, fine linens are replaced by coarse sackcloth, beautifying cosmetics of oil and myrrh are replaced by doleful ashes, and decadent foods are replaced by a sober fast.

In his distress, Mordecai goes up to the entrance of the king's gate to get the attention of Esther and, for the second time after learning of a murderous plot, to use her as an intermediary to reach the king. But he is not able to enter. Persian kings did not like to have their merry world disturbed, and so no one wearing mourning garments of sackcloth is allowed past that point. Therefore, Mordecai is not able to communicate face-to-face with Esther.

## MORDECAI APPEALS TO ESTHER (4:4–8)

Nevertheless, Esther's young maids and eunuchs find out about the scene that Mordecai is making outside the king's gate and hurry off to tell the queen. Once informed, Esther too becomes deeply distressed. She apparently does not know at this point what is troubling him, but given the fact that he's wearing sackcloth, she does know that something terrible must have happened.

Initially, she attempts to send a change of clothes to Mordecai, but he refuses them. He is apparently too distressed to think of removing his sackcloth. So the two of them are forced to remain separated from each other. Esther is inside and cannot leave the harem; Mordecai is outside and cannot get past the king's gate. The only recourse, then, is to employ an intermediary to carry messages back and forth between them. Only the most trusted confidant will do, so Esther calls for a eunuch named Hathach, who was one of the king's eunuchs appointed to attend to her. That the king would appoint him to look after the queen is a testimony to just how trustworthy he is. Having called him, Esther tells him to go back to the gate and find out exactly what is upsetting Mordecai.

Hathach does precisely what Esther instructs him to do. He goes outside the king's gate, into the open square (a traditional place of mourning), and finds Mordecai. Mordecai tells him everything that has happened—that Haman became infuriated and decided to put to death all the Jews of the empire, convinced the king to send out an edict to do so, and even promised an exorbitant sum of money to make it happen. How Mordecai could possibly have known the exact amount of silver promised to the king's treasury is not revealed, but Mordecai does always seem to have his ear to the ground when it comes to murderous scheming within the palace walls. Nevertheless, the fact that Mordecai wants Esther to know exactly how much money was put up by Haman is no doubt Mordecai's way of ensuring that she knows just how grave this situation really is. Then he produces a copy of the text of the edict, so that Hathach can take it to Esther and let her read it with her own eyes. Finally, Mordecai tells him, "Please urge her not to stand by idly or to look the other way. Please tell her to step in and help us. Tell her to go to the king and beg for mercy—to do whatever she has to do, but help us!"

## A DEFINING MOMENT (4:9–17)

Hathach returns to Esther and tells her everything that Mordecai has told him. Esther has some reservations, though. She certainly knows how risky it is for someone to enter the king's throne room uninvited and to begin making demands of the king. Persian law was very strict on that sort of thing. A king had to have privacy and protection. Only seven highly trusted officials could enter without first being summoned by the king. Anyone else who tried that would be put to death, unless pardoned by the king. Esther was not one of the seven.

Complicating the matter is the fact that if Esther goes to the king to make an appeal for her people, she will be forced to reveal that she is a Jew, which up to this point she has been hiding. As poorly as Ahasuerus responds to disobedient wives, his reaction could be expected to be even worse for a wife who is not only disobedient but also deceptive.

Moreover, Ahasuerus has already shown that he has a short fuse, especially when it comes to his wife going against his orders. At the beginning of the story, Queen Vashti would not come when she was summoned. Now Queen Esther would be coming when she has not been summoned. If the past is any indication of the future, the reaction of the king would probably be severe. Esther could probably expect Ahasuerus either to have her put to death or to get rid of her, just as he did with Vashti, and seek a new wife.

In fact, the narrator has already hinted at the king's propensity to do just that. In chapter 2, the narrator mentions that there was a second gathering of virgins when Mordecai discovered the assassination plot of two of the king's eunuchs. That detail has long puzzled commentators because it is not immediately apparent how it advances the plot of the story. However, as Elizabeth Groves has persuasively argued,

> The allusion in 2.19a to a second gathering of virgins that had already taken place during the years between Esther's coronation and the terrifying decision she faced in ch. 4 serves as a signal, a reminder, to the audience that Esther's position of influence over King Ahasuerus was tenuous. In combination with other hints imbedded in the text, 2.19a serves to make the audience uncomfortably aware that Ahasuerus did not regard Esther with the boundless esteem that would be necessary to outweigh his rage at her direct defiance of Persian law.[4]

In other words, another gathering of virgins after she was made queen would have certainly made Esther fully aware that Ahasuerus was not opposed to seeking out other women. He had already done so. Would there really be any reason to think that a breach in protocol on her part would not be met with dismissal or death and another search for a new queen?

Exacerbating that fear is Esther's own awareness that she has not been summoned by the king for the last thirty days (and certainly such a self-indulgent king hasn't been sleeping alone all that time). Clearly, she would seem to have little relational leverage with the king at this point. She has no heartstrings to pull. She has only his temper to enrage.

All in all, the odds are heavily stacked against her. Nothing would indicate that an uninvited entrance into the throne room would go well. Persian law forbids it. The concealment of her identity complicates it. The impulsiveness of the king threatens it.

Esther is now in a defining moment. She can either retreat into self-protective silence or she can take the ultimate risk, hold her breath, and go into the throne room. The first option may save her own neck, but her people will be ruthlessly slaughtered. The second option may save her people, but it risks her own death to do so. Even then, it may not save her people. Haman's edict has been issued; could it really be revoked?

People of faith frequently find themselves in similar situations, even if the stakes are not always as high. How they respond often reveals much about their faith and about what kind of character they have. A girl is mistreated at school, and a Christian classmate finds herself in a defining moment. Will she retreat in self-protective silence and slink away, or will she identify with her classmate and come to her aid? The first is the easier route; it saves her own neck, while letting the other person take the abuse. The second option is riskier. She may come to the aid of the mistreated classmate, but she risks her own reputation to do it.

Suppose that something unethical is taking place at a company. Customers, shareholders, or employees are being cheated in the process. A Christian employee finds himself in a defining moment. Will he retreat in self-protective silence and look the other way, or will he stand up and speak for those who are being unknowingly victimized? The first protects his self-interest, while letting others continue to pay the price for it. The second is much riskier. Blowing the whistle or confronting the wrongdoers may very well mean the loss of his employment, reputation, and income. Even then, his chances of success, like Esther's chances, may be low; his efforts may not benefit the victims in the end—but it is still the right thing to do.

Suppose a Christian finds herself in a situation where she can benefit financially in a significant way. The problem is that she will have to compromise her integrity. Maybe it means filing her taxes in a way that is less than honest. Maybe there is a business opportunity that bends the rules. Maybe there is a chance to do some creative accounting that, strictly speaking, is not entirely legal. Or perhaps she stumbles into a chance to play an insurance company for her own advantage. She too is in a defining moment. She can either compromise for her own benefit, while other policyholders, taxpayers, or citizens assume the cost for it, or she can do the right thing at personal financial cost. The first is easier, and she can probably rationalize it by saying that the cost will be spread so thin that no one will even feel the difference. But the second is the way of character and integrity.

Suppose, due to a careless mistake, an organization faces some unfortunate or unintended ramifications. The leader faces a defining moment. Will he throw those beneath him under the bus, letting them take the fall while he saves his own skin, or will he stand up and take responsibility for what has happened, even if it means great personal cost to his own career? The first option is expedient, but the second is responsible.

Suppose a friend or acquaintance is going through a difficult personal crisis. Once again, a Christian finds himself in a defining moment. Getting involved will require significant personal sacrifice on his part, but it will benefit the other person tremendously. Will he step in to the other person's life and identify himself with his friend, even when it will cost him much in time, energy, and perhaps even money? Or will he withdraw and tell himself that surely help will arise from another place?

Esther is in that kind of defining moment; she is at a fork in the road. Either she can try to save her own neck while her people perish, or she can risk her own life, hoping to save theirs. Knowing the difficulty of the situation, Mordecai sends back a report with several lines of argument to encourage her to do the right thing. He begins by saying, "Do not think to yourself that in the king's palace you will escape any more than all the other Jews" (4:13). In other words, if Esther chooses to remain silent in order to try to play it safe, it will not benefit her in the end. She is a Jew, and the edict makes no distinctions between Jews inside the palace and Jews outside the palace. According to the edict, all Jews are to be put to death—no exceptions. Thus, if Esther does the right thing by interceding with the king on behalf of her people, she does put herself at risk. She might keep her life; she might not. But if she does not go to the king and keeps quiet instead, then she may keep her life for now, but in the end will surely die. In other words, she is a Jew, just like all the other Jews in the empire, and her only hope is the same as their only hope: she must take the risk of going to the king and pleading with him on behalf of her people.

Then he continues, "For if you keep silent at this time, relief and deliverance will rise for the Jews from another place, but you and your father's family will perish" (v. 14).[5] Some have supposed that Mordecai is making a veiled threat to Esther, letting her know that if she will not try to intercede with the king for her people, he will reveal her true identity to the authorities. However, Mordecai has shown only care, concern, and love toward Esther. More likely, Mordecai is trying to emphasize to her that, ultimately, doing the wrong thing is no safer than doing the right thing, and that he has faith that relief and deliverance will ultimately come from somewhere, if not from her. Perhaps Mordecai is thinking of other Jewish officials within the palace, Persian officials who are sympathetic to the Jews, an external political power, or some other intervention. However, he leaves the potential source vague, only affirming his confidence that it will arise from another place, if necessary.

Mordecai then closes his appeal with a challenging question. "Who knows whether you have not come to the kingdom for such a time as this?" (v. 14). The looming day of slaughter had been determined by "chance," by the casting of lots. But Mordecai suggests to Esther that she may very well not be in her current position by chance or accident. Perhaps there is something larger, something purposeful and providential, at work. Perhaps she wasn't gathered into the palace with all the other virgins by chance. Perhaps she didn't just happen to appeal to the king. Perhaps the fact that she, a Jew, is the queen at this particular point in time is not accidental at all. Perhaps God has placed her right where she is, in this very place, in this defining moment, so that she might be the means through which her people are delivered. Perhaps there is something larger at work than Agagite hatred and the fate of the lots; perhaps there is a deeper providential plan at work that has placed Esther in this fortuitous position, for just such a time as this.

As a result, Esther responds with conviction. She sends a reply back to Mordecai: "Go, gather all the Jews to be found in Susa, and hold a fast on my behalf, and do not eat or drink for three days, night or day. I and my young women will also fast as you do. Then I will go to the king, though it is against the law, and if I perish, I perish" (v. 16). So while the king and Haman are feasting, Esther and the Jews begin fasting. The Jews have already begun to fast at the news of the terrible edict, but now Esther requests that they hold an intercessory fast on her behalf. And it is a particularly severe fast. Many fasts were only during the day; this was day and night. Moreover, it was three days long. Not only that, but this fast would begin on the eve of Passover, thus interfering with the all-important celebration.[6] However, desperate times call for desperate measures. After three days, she will go to the king, come what may. If she lives, she lives; if she perishes, she perishes.

Significantly, Esther has been transformed in the crucible of crisis. For the first time, Esther is not just passively floating downstream in the current of Persian culture; she is willing to swim upstream to do what is right. She no longer just accepts whatever Mordecai tells her to do, but, for the first time, takes action and tells Mordecai what to do. In fact, up to this point, Esther has been the object, not the subject, of most verbs, and has not spoken one word in the story. But from now on, "she is a shrewd and able figure, initiating the action, able to execute her plans, obtain royal favor, and defeat her people's enemy."[7]

In this defining moment, Esther for the first time responds with resolute conviction, declaring, "I will go, and if I perish, I perish." For the first time, she acts with courage and not compromising compliance. For the first time, doing what is right is more important to her than her own well-being. All of it is brought out because Mordecai has urged her to see herself as part of a larger providential plan, to realize that the circumstances that have brought her to this moment have not been random or accidental, but rather have been orchestrated to give her a crucial and indispensible role to play in their people's deliverance. Consequently, her distressing moment of crisis becomes for her a defining moment of conviction.

## DEFINING MOMENTS AND GOD'S PROVIDENTIAL WORK

Esther's defining moment is but a shadow of the greatest defining moment in the history of the world—though it took place, not at a Persian gate, but in a Palestinian garden. There, in the shadows of night, all eternity was condensed into a single moment of truth. The fate of the world and its history lay as a fork in the road before one man. If he retreated, he would save his own skin, but the whole world would perish in its sin. However, if he put his own life on the line, it would mean the salvation and deliverance of God's people. The first would have been easier, but the second was the will of his heavenly Father.

Jesus was even greater in his defining moment than Esther was in hers. Esther became troubled in the midst of her defining moment, but Jesus became sorrowful even unto death (Matt. 26:38). Esther called out to her people for a fast from table and cup, but Jesus called out to his heavenly Father, "If it be possible, let this cup pass from me" (Matt. 26:39). Esther asked her fellow Jews to join with her day and night, and they did, but Jesus asked his followers to join with him for only one hour during the night, and they fell asleep (Matt. 26:38, 40–41, 43). Esther took up sackcloth and ashes, entering into death symbolically, but

Jesus took up the beams and the nails, entering into death literally.[8] Esther responded in her defining moment with the knowledge that she *might* perish, but Jesus responded with the knowledge that he *would* perish.

Yet, despite his great sorrow, despite the excruciating pain before him, despite the fickle abandonment by his followers, despite the knowledge of certain death, Jesus did not retreat into self-protective avoidance. He did not cower in weakness. He did not opt for the path of least resistance. No, when Jesus faced his defining moment, having been called by God in the fullness of time for such a time as this, he responded with resolute conviction and courage, "Not my will, but yours, be done" (Luke 22:42). With courage, he walked into the crucible of the cross, knowing that he would certainly perish, that there would be no golden scepter extended for his escape, and he did so knowing that, in his perishing, God would accomplish the deliverance of his people—a salvation much greater than the deliverance from the edict of Haman, a salvation from the judgments of sin, death, and evil.

As a result, our own defining moments should be seen with a new perspective. To begin with, in the same way that Esther was challenged by Mordecai, we too must be challenged to see our defining moment in its larger context. As Mordecai pointed out to Esther, doing the wrong thing may pay off in the short term, but it never pays off in the long run. We may save ourselves from social ridicule, we may keep our job, we may make a little money, we may evade the blame in the organizational shake-up, we may avoid the cost of caring for a friend, but it will always cost us in the end. As Mordecai also pointed out, we must realize that if we are not willing to do what God has called us to do in our defining moment, God will still accomplish his purposes through alternative means—but we will miss out on being a part of what he's doing, not only in the situation, but in our own lives as well.

This truth was powerfully realized by William Wilberforce, the eighteenth- and nineteenth-century English politician who spearheaded the abolition of the African slave trade in England. In the late eighteenth century, contrary to popular views of the time, England was an extremely degraded society, morally speaking, and traditional Christianity was generally dismissed as quaint and fanatical. Much of the clergy had jettisoned orthodox Christian doctrine, and preachers like John Newton, John Wesley, and George Whitefield were the exception, not the rule. By and large, the country had became spiritually asleep and morally dead. The inhuman and deplorable West Indies slave trade, with its infamous "Middle Passage," was only one expression, though one of the worst, of the larger moral ills of the society at the time.

Though exposed to "serious Christianity" (as it was called) during his childhood, through a godly aunt and uncle, Wilberforce did not have a personal faith in Christ until he was in his twenties and already serving in Parliament. Beginning to study Scripture carefully, he became distraught over the moral evil of slavery. Initially, he thought that he had to leave politics in order to be a faithful Christian. But others encouraged him to think differently, to see his position in Parliament as the means through which he could effect change. After spending significant time considering the issue, on May 12, 1787, Wilberforce went to visit his good friend, who was also the prime minister, William Pitt, at his country home, Holwood Estate. Joining them was Pitt's cousin, William Grenville, who would eventually succeed Pitt as prime minister. During their conversation under an old oak tree, Pitt charged Wilberforce, "Do not lose time, or the ground will be occupied by another." As one of his biographers describes it, "What Pitt said was true enough, for if, as Wilberforce thought, God Himself was calling him to this task and he shrank from it, God too could find another to do it, and surely would."[9] But Wilberforce did not shrink from the task before him. He became convinced that God had raised him up "for such a time as this," to bring to an end the inhuman treatment of countless men, women, and children; and if he were to fail to act, God would surely find someone else to fulfill this vital calling. From that moment on, Wilberforce faced his calling boldly and determined to be faithful in the midst of his own defining moment. As a result of his relentless, enduring, and faithful efforts over the next several decades, the terrible practice of human enslavement was abolished in England.

In the same way, when we find ourselves in a crucible of testing or a difficult crisis, as Esther found herself and as Wilberforce found himself, we should not focus primarily on how we can get out of the difficulty we are in, leaving "the ground" to be "occupied by another"; instead, we should focus mainly on the fact that God has placed us for his purposes exactly where we are at this defining moment—"for such a time as this"—and then ask how God might want to use us in that situation. That means that we need to ask ourselves, "Why might God have placed me in this neighborhood, with these neighbors, at this point in time?" "Why might God have placed me in this office, with these coworkers, during this season of this company's life and during these seasons of my colleagues' lives?" "Why might God have crossed my path with this person's path at this moment in time? How might he want to use me in her life?" "Why might God have placed us in this country, at this point in history, in the midst of these events? What would faithfulness to him look like here and now? What might he want to do with us and through us in our community, in our schools, in our businesses, in our churches, in our nation, and in our world?" "Why has God placed me exactly where he has me right now? What are the defining moments at this stage in my life?"

Having adjusted our perspective to see our defining moment as orchestrated by the providential hand of God for his purposes, we must then face that defining moment with a willingness to lose everything to follow Christ, knowing that Christ himself, in his defining moment, was willing to lose everything for us. For Esther, realizing that her life was being guided by the hand of providence meant being willing to risk her own life to try to save her people. As Michael Fox has written, "Esther's life just might be more significant than she realizes. It might hold a meaning she has not envisioned. For that very reason she must be willing to risk it."[10] For us, realizing that our life is providentially bound up with the crucified and risen Christ means a willingness to lose everything to follow him. It means being willing to sacrifice everything in this life for the sake of the true life that Jesus gives. As Jesus himself said,

> If anyone would come after me, let him deny himself and take up his cross and follow me. For whoever would save his life will lose it, but whoever loses his life for my sake will find it. For what will it profit a man if he gains the whole world and forfeits his soul? Or what shall a man give in return for his soul? For the Son of Man is going to come with his angels in the glory of his Father, and then he will repay each person according to what he has done. (Matt. 16:24–27)

With the conviction and courage of Esther, the young lady in the midst of a defining moment at school can say to herself, "Because Jesus has already gone to the cross for me and suffered ostracism for my sake, I will come to this student's side, and if I'm ostracized, I'm ostracized." The businessman in the midst of a defining moment in the workplace can say, "Because Jesus has already gone to the cross for me and suffered rejection for my sake, I will do the right thing, and if I'm fired, I'm fired." The woman with an unethical opportunity for financial gain can say, "Because Jesus has already gone to the cross for me and suffered loss for my sake, I will act with integrity, and if

I suffer loss, I suffer loss." The leader of an organization in the midst of a defining moment that requires someone to take responsibility for a mess that's been created can say, "Because Jesus has already gone to the cross for me and stepped into my place of judgment, I will step up and take responsibility, and if my career is wrecked, my career is wrecked." The man facing a defining moment because his friend is in a crisis can say, "Because Jesus has already gone to the cross for me and come to my aid at great personal cost, I will come to my friend's aid, and if it costs me greatly, it costs me greatly." Whatever the defining moment, we can act with conviction and courage by saying, "I too will cast myself into the hands of my God, for these are the hands that have already received the cup of bitterness in the garden of Gethsemane. These are the hands that have already taken up the nails on the cross of Calvary. These are the hands that have already been at work underneath me and around me and beside me, so that I might respond with courage and conviction in this very moment and say, 'Who knows? This place. This time. This situation. This position. Maybe, just maybe, God has placed me right where I am for just such a time as this.' "

In the years leading up to the Second World War and the rise of Nazism in Germany, the pastor and writer Dietrich Bonhoeffer was confronted with his own defining moment. On November 9–10, 1938, paramilitary soldiers and civilians aligned with the Nazi Party executed a series of coordinated attacks known as Kristallnacht (meaning "crystal night," referring to the shattered glass that covered the streets after the attacks). Jewish homes, schools, and hospitals were raided, more than one thousand synagogues were burned, and more than seven thousand Jewish businesses were destroyed. Nearly one hundred Jews were killed, and thirty thousand Jews were detained and sent to concentration camps. Meanwhile, German authorities stood by and did nothing to stop it.

In the aftermath, many in Germany found themselves in a defining moment. Were they to look the other way in order to protect themselves from danger, while letting thousands of others perish, or were they to step forward in protest, at considerable personal risk? At first, it looked as though Dietrich Bonhoeffer might choose the former and keep silent, but he began moving toward courageous action.[11] His friend, Eberhard Bethge, notes that Bonhoeffer made a significant note in his Bible. In fact, it was the only marginal note in Bonhoeffer's Bible that was not a reference to a parallel passage or a related hymn. Next to Psalm 74:8, he wrote, "9.11.38"—that is, November 9, 1938, the day of the Kristallnacht attacks. The verse itself reads, "They said to themselves, 'We will utterly subdue them'; they burned all the meeting places of God in the land." The next two verses read, "We do not see our signs; there is no longer any prophet, and there is none among us who knows how long. How long, O God, is the foe to scoff? Is the enemy to revile your name forever?" As it turns out, that was the passage that Bonhoeffer and his students had been reading that very day in their secret seminary. For Bonhoeffer, it was impossible to miss the similarities between the destructive attacks that the Jews faced at the hands of the Babylonians and those that they were facing in his own day in Germany.

A few days later, he circulated a letter to all the former students of the seminary. The letter had already been prepared before the events of Kristallnacht, but Bonhoeffer inserted one sentence: "During the last few days, I have been thinking a lot about Psalm 74, Zechariah 2:8, Romans 9:3f., and 11:11–15. That really makes one pray." Commenting on this inserted sentence in the letter, Bethge writes, "It seems to me that Bonhoeffer's attention was caught by the double 'how long' of Psalm 74. When will there be an end to the pogrom? How will the end come about? What role will fall to me in it?" As events unfolded, Dietrich Bonhoeffer came to believe that he did have a role to play, that he had been providentially placed where he was for just such a time as this, that this was his defining moment, and that faithfulness meant opposing the Nazis and Hitler as they sought to destroy the Jewish people in his own land.

During the course of our lives, each of us finds ourselves confronted by defining moments, moments in which we, like Esther, have before us a fork in the road. We can either choose to do the right thing at great personal risk or choose to do the expedient thing for our own benefit, despite the cost to others. In such moments, our calling is to trust by faith that God's providential hand has placed us just where we are, for such a time as this, and then to set our hearts upon the one who gave himself for us. For if our hearts are set on him and his love for us on the cross, we will be able to take up our cross and follow him, no matter what crisis we face or what crucible of testing we are in.

## FOR FURTHER REFLECTION

1. When have you found yourself in a defining moment? What risks were there?
2. What factors made it difficult to act with courageous faith?
3. Did you act or not? What did you learn from acting or not acting that will shape how you respond in future defining moments?
4. How could remembering what Jesus did for you in his own defining moment have empowered you to act with courageous faith? How is it good news for you as you recall times when you failed to act with courageous faith?

CHAPTER SIX

# STEP OF FAITH (5:1–8)

*You want always to see through Providence, do you not? You never will, I assure you. . . . Honor God by trusting Him. (Charles Haddon Spurgeon*[1]*)*

At Mordecai's urging, Esther has decided to go to the king to intervene on behalf of her people. In preparation, she, her attendants, and the Jews in Susa have been fasting night and day for three days. Just as she prepared herself physically, with special food, to win the king's favor the first time, so now she has prepared herself spiritually, by fasting from food, to win the king's favor the second time.[2]

## ESTHER APPROACHES THE KING'S QUARTERS (5:1)

Having gone through three days of fasting, Esther has naturally picked up some physical symptoms. She likely looks weary and has lost some weight. After three days of food deprivation, the change in her appearance would not be dramatic, but perhaps still noticeable, even if it has been several weeks since the king has seen her. Normally, such a change in appearance would be a disadvantage. Unlike in our culture, it was generally considered more attractive in the ancient world to be full in figure.[3] That is why the girls auditioning to be the next queen were given not just beauty treatments, but also special food. The purpose in supplying cosmetics and delicacies was to make them more attractive to the king. However, Esther has been fasting from food and water for three days and is probably beginning to show some thinning, which certainly will not help her, given that she is approaching a king who has already shown that physical appearance is extremely important to him.

That isn't the only strike against her. As she has already emphasized to Mordecai, going to the king without being summoned was against Persian law. According to the law, anyone other than the king's seven highly trusted officials who came before the king without a summons would receive the penalty of death. In fact, some reliefs from the Persian period show Persian kings sitting on their throne holding a scepter and flanked by a soldier holding an ax, ready to execute any uninvited visitors to the throne room.[4] Only if the king extended his golden scepter would the violator be pardoned. Esther, of course, is well aware of court protocol and knows that her only hope is that the king will extend the scepter, so that the guard will not extend his ax.

Consequently, the plan to go before the king must have been extraordinarily frightening for young Esther. Physically speaking, she has been fasting for three days. Relationally, she has not been summoned for the last thirty days, but now will be revealing to him that she has been deceiving him for five years by hiding her Jewish identity. Historically, Ahasuerus has not reacted well to a wife who disregards his decrees. In fact, the narrator seems to drive home just how intimidating it was by using the words for "king" and "royal" (which share a common Hebrew root) six times in the first verse of chapter 5 alone. It is as if the narrator is piling up references to royalty to emphasize the magnitude of the authority that Esther will be confronting.

In light of what she is facing, Esther takes great care in preparing herself before going. Previously, she needed a eunuch to guide her in her preparations; now she has the wisdom to know what to wear.[5] She very wisely decides to put on her royal robes. Unlike her first time going to the king, she does not go this time to seduce, but to talk about a serious and formal matter. So she puts on her royal robes and, by doing so, shrewdly presents herself as someone with a high status, hoping thereby to communicate implicitly to Ahasuerus that he should treat her accordingly, that is, with dignity and honor.

Then she begins her fateful walk to the inner court of the king. Of course, she does not know—cannot know—what the outcome will be when the king sees her. She does not know whether the king will be in a generous mood or an irritable mood. She does not know whether she will make a good impression on him or not. She does not know whether she will find favor with him or not. Nevertheless, with courage, conviction, and perhaps some faith, she goes.

Most people of faith have had a similar experience, stepping out with courage, conviction, and perhaps some faith—even if that faith is weak or tenuous—not really knowing what will happen when they do. Taking the step, they do not know—cannot know—whether things will end up going well for them or whether it will turn out to be a disaster. They do not know whether it will "pay off" or whether it will cost them.

For instance, a college graduate senses that God is calling him into campus ministry. He turns down lucrative job offers and a comfortable life, taking his college debt and trying to raise his financial support. His family and friends tell him he is making a terrible mistake, that he is throwing away his education, that he will regret it later. But he has a deep conviction that God is leading him to step out in faith. He believes that God desires to use him in the lives of college students. So he begins the journey, courageously following God's calling, but ultimately not knowing whether his financial needs will be met or not.

A woman is forced out of her job because she refuses to engage in dubious practices. She knows that she must leave if she is to keep her integrity, but she does not have another job offer in hand. She is given a meager severance package, and she has some savings, but she has no way of knowing whether she will find another job quickly or not. The future to her is blind, and she must walk into the dark courageously, not knowing whether things will work out for her or not.

A married man with children decides to go back to school to get an advanced degree. He believes that he needs the training he will get. His wife and children support his decision and are ready for the transition. However, he lies awake, night after night, second-guessing whether he is doing the right thing. In his heart, he believes that he is. He has tried to cover all the angles and to be as wise as possible. But ultimately he does not know for sure whether this will turn out to be the best decision he has ever made or the worst. He can only hold his breath and step out in faith.

A young couple sense God leading them to adopt a child from overseas. The details, the cultural barriers, and all the unknowns of the process seem overwhelming. They do not know whether their new child will turn out to have major health problems or significant disabilities. They do not know whether they will make several trips and become attached to their new child, only to have the home country's government pull the rug out from under them at the last moment. They do not know what challenges may await them because they will now be a multiethnic family. They do not know whether this child, down the road, will fill them with pride or fill them with pain. But they have a conviction deep within their hearts that they are being called to step out in faith and pursue this adoption.

Taking steps like these can be almost paralyzing with fear. What will happen? Are we mistaking presumption for conviction and foolishness for faith? What if things don't work out? What if we crash and burn? What if our hearts are broken? What if we suffer significant loss? What if something happens that we were not expecting and could not plan for? What if we go through all this and have nothing to show for it? What if we end up looking back years later with an overwhelming sense of regret and no way to remedy it? As these questions roll around in our heads, we may find that sleep is elusive, anxiety is a constant struggle, and fear becomes a constant feeling. But there is no way to make the unknown known. All we can do is step out in faith, despite not knowing how things will unfold or whether the risk will pay off.

In a similar way, Esther must step out in faith, even though she does not know what the outcome will be and the personal risk is great. However, even though she must step out in faith, she acts as shrewdly as she can. She goes to the edge of the inner court, in front of the king's hall, and stands there. Wisely, she does not barge in; she just stands at the very edge of the court, doing just enough to get in the king's line of sight and then waiting for him to notice her, hoping that her reserve and discretion will win her his welcome. In taking this approach, Esther shows a wise balance between bold faith and thoughtful planning.

## ESTHER REQUESTS A FEAST (5:2–5)

At some point, the king notices Esther standing in the court. As she waits for his response, Esther must be holding her breath. How will the king react to seeing her in the court uninvited? Then, relief! When he sees her, the king's reaction is favorable. Literally, she "won favor in his sight." The idiom is the same as the one used when Esther won the favor of the eunuch during Ahasuerus's search for a new queen. Just as in that situation, the sense is that she was active ("won favor") and not passive ("found favor"). That is, her shrewd tactics have worked just as she hoped. Her decision to clothe herself in her royal robes and exercise discretion and restraint in standing in the court opposite the entrance to the throne room has made the king favorably disposed to her. As a result, he extends the golden scepter and allows her to approach the throne.

No doubt Esther breathes a great sigh of relief. However, she could still anger the king when she makes her request. The king could easily become infuriated that she has been concealing her ethnic identity from him, thus putting him in a most difficult position in light of his previous approval of Haman's edict. Similarly, the king could just as easily become angered as well by the perceived audacity of the queen to suggest that he overturn a law that he has authorized.

So she approaches the throne and touches the tip of the scepter. The king asks her, "What is it, Queen Esther? What is your request?" Surely it is a good sign that the king refers to her as his queen and warmly invites her request. Then, in typical ancient Near Eastern hyperbole, he adds, "It shall be given you, even to the half of my kingdom." In other words, "I'm predisposed to being gracious to you, so whatever your request is, tell it to me." The irony is comical: the king "has so far spoken only twice: once, when he gave his consent to the annihilation of all the Jews, and now, when he makes a present of sixty-three and a half provinces to a woman who, unknown to him, is a Jewess!"[6] Not surprisingly, given his characteristic rashness, Ahasuerus gives Esther a virtual blank check, just as he gave to Haman earlier.

Of course, Esther could state her request right here and now, but she has a much better idea, one that will effectively force the king to grant her request. She invites the king to come to a banquet this very day that she has already prepared and says that she would like Haman to come too. The request seems reasonable enough—and this king does love to feast!—so the king orders that Haman be called so that they can go together to Esther's banquet.

This provides a subtle indication within the narrative that power is shifting.[7] Up until this point, Esther has always come into the king's space, at his bidding. Initially, she won his favor by entering his bedroom. Then she won his favor and entered the throne room to make her request. But now the situation is reversed. Esther is the hostess and the king (and Haman) will enter her space, at her bidding. Ever so subtly, the power is shifting to Esther; from now on, she will be the one steering the events. This impression is reinforced by the fact that, with one exception, Esther has been referred to simply as "Esther" up until this point; from now on, she will almost always be referred to as "Queen Esther." Perhaps the king's insinuation that half the kingdom rightly belongs to her is less hyperbolic than even he realizes at this point!

## ESTHER REQUESTS A SECOND FEAST (5:6–8)

After the king and Haman have eaten their fill of Esther's prepared food and they are drinking wine after the feast, the king asks her again, "What is your wish? It shall be granted you. And what is your request? Even to the half of my kingdom, it shall be fulfilled."

Esther begins, "My petition and my request is . . ."—but then she breaks it off. Instead she says, "If the king regards me with favor, and if it pleases the king to grant my petition and fulfill my request, let the king and Haman come tomorrow to the banquet I will prepare for them. Then I will answer the king's question." The reader's question, of course, is why Esther invites them to a second banquet. She clearly has both the king's favor and his ear. Why does she not capitalize on the moment and offer her request while she has the opportunity? Some have suggested that she sensed it was not the right moment. Others have suggested that she simply lost her nerve and deferred it another day to give herself a chance to gain more courage. But perhaps there is something else going on. After all, the king really does seem to be predisposed to granting her request, so it seems strange that Esther would think it is not the right moment or that she would lose her nerve when everything else in this passage suggests that she is poised and in control. A better suggestion is that this is actually another shrewd move by Esther. The wording of the second invitation is the key. She says, "If it pleases the king to grant my petition, then come tomorrow to another banquet." In other words, Esther effectively ties together the king's attendance at the second banquet, which would be easy to do and almost impossible to refuse, with an advance commitment to grant the request. Just by showing up, the king will have already implicitly committed himself to grant whatever request Esther makes of him.

Moreover, she also shrewdly sets it up so that Haman will be there too. After all, he is the mastermind behind the planned slaughter, and she will need him there for the confrontation. If Haman were not there, the king could agree verbally, but then, when he is with his counselors later—and he's already shown that he is extremely malleable in their hands—he could be persuaded to change his mind in her absence. However, by arranging a second feast in the way that she does, she both locks in the king's permission for whatever she will ask and makes it virtually binding by having Haman be present for it. After all, this is a very proud king, and he certainly will not want to lose face by granting something in front of his chief official and then reversing it later.

Yet the outcome is clearly not just a product of Esther's shrewdness. Even with all her shrewdness, the king did not have to extend the scepter, but he did. The king did not have to invite a request, but he did. The king did not have to come to the banquet, but he did. The king did not have to insist that Haman come along, as Esther wanted, but he did. The king did not have to agree to a second banquet, but he did. The reason, of course, is that, as the book of Proverbs says, "The king's heart is a stream of water in the hand of the LORD; he turns it wherever he will" (Prov. 21:1). Persian kings are not exempt.

In Esther's case, she trusts in the providence that has brought her to this place for such a time as this, and she acts accordingly. When she does, she discovers something remarkable. She has thought out her plan carefully. She has prepared it well. She executes it with perfect poise and shrewdness. But in the midst of all her efforts, there is something beyond her efforts, which is guiding the king and his response to her. What she cannot see, but which has nevertheless been happening through it all, is that God has been at work through her courage, her boldness, and her shrewdness. God has been at work to make her reception before the king warm and her appeal to the king successful. God is at work, guiding events with his invisible hand according to his larger purposes.

## STEPPING OUT IN FAITH

Never was there a greater act of faith in the face of certain doom than on Calvary. Throughout Jesus' life and ministry, his sights were set on the cross. There he would willingly die on behalf of his people. There his faithfulness to his heavenly Father would reach its consummate fulfillment. There he would act with utmost faith, even as he stared into the dark and horrifying abyss of death. Yet, when he arrived at that crucial moment, the hands of his Father, on which he so constantly depended, seemed to withdraw. When he looked up, his Father looked away. When he cried out for his Father, all he could detect was a profound and devastating forsakenness. He would have to face death and take this final step of faithfulness into the terrifying abyss all alone. And yet, as Luke records, his final words were the ultimate step of faith in the face of sure and certain doom, entrusting himself to the Father who had forsaken him and to the hands that had withdrawn from him. "Jesus, calling out with a loud voice, said, 'Father, into your hands I commit my spirit!' And having said this he breathed his last" (Luke 23:46).

Later, Luke repeatedly records that those very same hands into which Jesus had committed his spirit faithfully raised up his body (Acts 2:24, 32; 3:15, 26; 4:10; 5:30; 10:40; 13:30, 34, 37). Now Jesus is at the right hand of God, an indication not only of Jesus' unfailing faithfulness to his Father, but also of his Father's faithfulness to him (Acts 7:55–56). Even in the midst of Jesus' anguished step of faith on the cross, God's purposes held firm and, ultimately, the Father's hands were there to receive his faithful servant.

Such is the case for his followers as well. The one who seeks to walk by faith must do so without the privilege of sight (2 Cor. 5:7). Steps of faith are always blind. Trust must precede confirmation. That, of course, can be terrifying. Yet God gives us the encouraging assurance of his faithful and providential hand. His hand may not order our circumstances exactly as we had hoped when we stepped out in faith. He may not cause matters to play out just as we had envisioned. But if we step out in faith with a pure heart (so far as that is possible), and do so in a sincere effort to follow his lead and to be faithful to his call (so far as we are able to determine it), then we can experience the comforting reassurance that God's providential hands will bear us up in the midst of whatever comes our way. Resting in his providence becomes our support as we step into the unknown. As R. C. Sproul has written, "The Providence of God is our fortress, our shield, and our very great reward. It is what provides courage and perseverance for His saints."[8]

And why shouldn't we take heart? Paul says in the book of Romans, "He who did not spare his own Son but gave him up for us all, how will he not also with him graciously give us all things?" (Rom. 8:32). In context, Paul is assuring us not that God will give us whatever we want but that God, in his sovereignty, will work all things for our good in the end (v. 28). We can be sure that he will arrange things in our lives such that we are increasingly conformed to the image of Christ himself (v. 29). We can be sure that God will providentially orchestrate things in our lives so that we are further sanctified and brought to our completion in Christ, which is eventual glorification (v. 30). Thus, no one can truly be against us (in an ultimate sense), no one can bring any charge against us (that will stick in God's ultimate courtroom), no one can condemn us (in terms of our eternal destiny), and nothing—absolutely nothing, not even tribulation or distress or persecution or famine or nakedness or danger or sword, not even death or life, or angels or rulers, or things present or things to come, or height or depth, or anything else in all creation—can separate us from the love of God in Christ Jesus our Lord (vv. 31–39).

With that bedrock of assurance in Christ's never-failing love and in God's gracious providence in our lives, we have all we need to step out in faith, wherever he may lead us. After all, as Paul says, if God would deliver up his own Son for us, then why would he abandon us when we need him most? Why would he fail us when we are seeking to follow him? Why would he prove himself faithless when we are taking steps of faith? No, the cross convinces us that the same God who loves us that much must also care enough about us to be right there with his faithful and providential hands beneath us when we step out in faith. And though, like Esther, we may not know exactly how things will turn out, or whether things will go the way we hope or not, we can step out in faith with the assurance that God's hands are bearing us up as we do.

Of course, like Esther, we must show a wise balance between bold faith and thoughtful planning. Esther was not foolish in her faith or reckless in her boldness. She took care to do whatever she could to win the king's favor. She put on royal robes. She showed a prudent sensibility by waiting in the inner court for the king to notice her before she entered the throne room. She cleverly held back her request and laid the groundwork first by preparing feasts for the king. She was bold in her faith, but she was thoughtful and careful at the same time.

We too must show the same balance between bold faith and thoughtful planning. The young man sensing a call to campus ministry must take care to make his calling sure. He must draw up a workable plan to support himself as he works to raise his financial support. While working, he must be diligent in the process, thinking through the specifics of how he will go about it and being faithful to do everything he can. He must consider practical matters like paying off student loans and obtaining proper medical insurance. Yes, he must step out in bold faith, trusting in God's providence, but he must do so with wisdom, care, and thoughtfulness, as Esther did.

The woman who faces a job loss because of her integrity needs to use her severance package in a frugal and shrewd way. She must do everything she can to put herself in the line of sight of possible employers and make every preparation she can to be appealing to them. Ultimately, she will have to trust God to open a new employment door for her and to provide for her needs in the meantime, but she must also diligently investigate every opportunity for new work that she can.

For the family man who plans to go back to school to get the training he needs, he must make sure, in conversation with his wife, that such a move is the best thing for their family and not just an expression of his own dissatisfactions or dreams, putting the family in a precarious position. He must do some realistic "budget math" and put together a plan that will get them through a lean period of time. They must count the cost and prepare themselves to adjust their standard of living in the interest of prudent stewardship.

The young couple desiring to adopt a child from overseas must also step out in faith, but they must take that step carefully They may need to do considerable research into the process beforehand. They may need to discuss at length what to expect with agencies and other people who have been through the process already. They need to give careful thought and make preparations, so far as they are able, for the unexpected and to discuss how they will handle the inevitable challenges they will face.

In other words, whether a young man is pursuing campus ministry, a woman is facing unemployment, a family man is considering going back to school, or a young couple is investigating a foreign adoption, humble faith is not the same as reckless presumption. Stepping out in faith is not a license to act foolishly and carelessly. We must be not only as innocent as doves, but also as shrewd as serpents (Matt. 10:16), at least as shrewd and prudent as everyone else in the world (Luke 16:1–13).

Yet, if we take steps of faith, with a sincere faith and godly wisdom, we do have the assurance that God's providential hands are there to catch us and guide us. Near the end of the movie *Indiana Jones and the Last Crusade*, Indiana Jones must go through three tests in order to reach the long-pursued and much-coveted Holy Grail. After overcoming the first two obstacles, he comes to a small opening, just small enough for his shoulders to squeeze through. He looks across to the other side, where there is another rocky wall, with another opening where the path continues. Looking down, he sees only a deep, dark abyss, and he can see no way to cross to the other side. Confused, he consults the Grail Diary in his hands and reads that he must jump. Looking back across the abyss, he says to himself, "Impossible! Nobody can jump this!" He looks down into the Diary again and he realizes that he must step out in faith. After steadying his nerves, he places his hand over his heart, takes a deep breath, and then steps off the cliff. For a brief moment, it looks as if he will fall to his death. Then, suddenly, his foot lands on something. It appears as if he is standing on an invisible bridge that is holding him up. As it turns out, the First Crusaders had ingeniously built the bridge in such a way that it perfectly blended into the rocky wall on the other side. When he leans to the side, the perfect visual alignment shifts and he can see the bridge stretching from one side to the other. It turns out that it was there all along. A rock-solid bridge was there to hold him up, but he could not see it and did not experience its reality until he stepped out in faith.

In the same way, we may not be able to see God's providential hands in front of us. The unknowns of our future may appear to be a deep, dark abyss. Like Esther, we may not know what awaits us or exactly how things will turn out. However, if we step out in faith, with a humble and trusting heart, we will find that God's providence was there all along. We may not be able to see it, but that does not mean that we cannot trust it—as Esther did when she took the treacherous walk to the king's inner court, and as Jesus himself did when he took his treacherous walk to the hill of Golgotha.

## FOR FURTHER REFLECTION

1. What are some ways in which you are called to step out in faith today? What makes it hard to do?
2. How do we know the difference between stepping out in faith and being presumptuous toward God? What distinguishes one from the other?
3. If we take steps of faith, what can we expect from God? What can we not necessarily expect?

CHAPTER SEVEN

# THE PIVOT POINT (5:9–6:14)

*In the infinite wisdom of the Lord of all the earth, each event falls with exact precision into its proper place in the unfolding of His divine plan. Nothing, however small, however strange, occurs without His ordering, or without its particular fitness for its place in the working out of His purpose. (B. B. Warfield[1])*

Esther has asked the king and Haman to come back the following day for a second banquet, where she will reveal her request to the king.

## HAMAN'S RAGE REKINDLED (5:9–15)

Feeling flattered for being invited to a private banquet with the king and queen, Haman goes out walking on air. He no doubt regards two exclusive banquets with the royal couple as a sure sign of his importance and his favor in their eyes.

However, his mood changes abruptly when he comes to the king's gate and sees his archenemy, Mordecai, there. Only a few days removed from the issuance of the edict, Mordecai not surprisingly has no love lost for Haman, and once again he shows no respect for him. In fact, he seems to have "escalated his noncompliance."[2] Previously he had refused to bow. Now he will not even rise or stir before him, as if he refuses to acknowledge Haman's presence altogether. Haman is infuriated.

Haman, of course, is already a proud man, but his ego must have been especially inflated after the king and queen invited him to a private royal banquet. It is no wonder that Mordecai's snub is especially infuriating at this particular moment. As quickly as he felt his pride stroked by the royal couple, he now feels it wounded by his most hated nemesis. Tellingly, his inflated pride not only makes him angry, but also keeps him from showing it. Apparently, he does not want Mordecai to know how much he is getting under his skin. So Haman keeps himself under control, bites his tongue, and goes home.

Still, it's eating at him. He just cannot stand this Mordecai. He hates everything about him. He hates him for being Jewish. He hates him for being disrespectful. He hates him for not giving him the glory and honor that he is certain he deserves. As a result, when he gets home, he gathers together his friends and his wife, Zeresh, and begins to boast to them about his vast wealth, his many sons, and all the honors and promotions he has received from the king. His bruised ego, full of anger and bitterness from the slight, needs to nurse itself with a recital of just how great he really is. Then he tells them something they do not yet know: that he is so great, so honorable, so important, that he has just come from a banquet with the king and the queen alone, and tomorrow he will dine with them again.

Nevertheless, boasting of his own greatness is still not enough to salve his wounded pride. All his honor, riches, fame, power, and importance are nothing if Mordecai is still there, silently and motionlessly mocking him at the gate. His ego is simply too fragile to let it lie. Sensing this, his wife and friends suggest that he build some gallows, fifty cubits high (approximately seventy-five feet), and then go to the king in the morning to secure his permission to hang Mordecai on it. That way he'll finally dispose of Mordecai and be able to go to the banquet with the king and the queen later in the day without it bothering him.

The suggestion is especially malicious. They don't just want to execute Mordecai; they want to humiliate him. For gallows to be seventy-five feet high is almost absurd, prompting some commentators to wonder if this is just ludicrous exaggeration. After all, the Persian palace was only about forty-five feet high. Other commentators have speculated that the gallows must have been built on a hill to achieve that kind of height. But clearly Haman, his wife, and his friends want this to be a very public execution, with Mordecai lifted high above the city so that everyone for miles around can see him up there.

Not only that, but in Persia gallows were used not to hang a person, as many people naturally assume, but to impale a person. In other words, the gallows would not have been a frame upon which a rope could be tied, but a large wooden stake. Given the grotesque nature of the execution, it was, not surprisingly, one of the most disgraceful ways a person could be executed and was typically reserved for sordid criminals, such as Bigthan and Teresh after they plotted to assassinate the king (Esth. 2:23). In sum, Haman and his entourage don't just want to execute Mordecai; they want to disgrace him, and to do it very publicly so that everyone in Susa can witness it. Mordecai had publicly humiliated him in Susa (3:2; 5:9); now he will publicly humiliate Mordecai there!

Already having proven his calloused bloodlust when offended, and not one to shy away from massive overkill in giving it an outlet, Haman loves the idea. Suddenly re-energized by the suggestion, he immediately conscripts some workers to begin construction, so that as soon as the stake is completed he can go straight to the king to ask for permission to kill Mordecai. How ironic it is that the very same man who has repeatedly been infuriated with Mordecai for violating the king's edict to pay homage to him is now himself, by following his wife's lead, in violation of the king's edict that every man in the empire should be the master in his own household (1:22)![3] However, it evidently never occurs to Haman. He is too delighted with her counsel and begins to follow it without delay.

At this point, it must seem as if nothing can go right. Just when it seems that Esther is catching her needed breaks and might actually succeed, Haman speeds up his attack on Mordecai. Esther is going to sit down with the king the next day, but now it appears that the next day might very well be too late for her cousin.

## THE KING DISCOVERS HIS OVERSIGHT (6:1–3)

Meanwhile, as the workers outside are feverishly working through the night on a giant stake, something else is going on inside the palace: the king is having trouble sleeping. As a remedy, he asks that someone bring in the administrative records to read to him. This would have been about as thrilling as reading a phone book, and having them read in the middle of the night would have been a good way to try to fall back asleep. Perhaps there is a touch of comedy here too: "If anything would send Ahasuerus back to sleep, it was surely the monotone reading of his own life story!"[4]

Opening the chronicles, the appointed reader just so happens to turn to the records of his reign from five years earlier and begins to read. As he reads, he relates how Mordecai thwarted an assassination attempt by two officials in the palace. However, the chronicle mentions nothing of any reward. The omission catches Ahasuerus's attention, and he asks what honor and recognition were given to Mordecai for what he had done. The attendants tell him that nothing has been done for him. Understandably, the king is concerned. It is not good for a king to let loyalty go unrewarded; his safety depends on it. Consequently, he feels a great urgency to rectify the oversight.

## THE HONORING OF MORDECAI (6:4–14)

At this very moment, the king hears someone out in the court. Turning to his attendants, he asks them who it is. As it turns out, it is Haman. He has come to secure the king's permission to execute Mordecai. But that Haman would arrive in the middle of the night reveals something interesting. His wife and friends had suggested that he have the gallows or stake built and then go to the king in the morning. But Haman has decided to come in the middle of the night, apparently so eager to execute Mordecai that he simply cannot wait until morning. Ironically, he happens to arrive right after the king has determined in his own mind to recognize and honor Mordecai. Also ironically, both the king and his top official cannot sleep, and one spends the midnight hours planning how he may honor Mordecai while the other spends those same hours planning how he may humiliate him.

Responding to the king's inquiry, his attendants inform him that it is Haman who is out in the court. Perfect! The king cannot seem to make a single decision without consultation, and who better to consult than his top official! What unfolds is something akin to Shakespeare's *The Comedy of Errors* or Abbott and Costello's "Who's on First?" The king has Haman brought in, and asks him what should be done for the man the king delights to honor—but in posing the question, the king just happens to omit the name of the man he intends to honor (just as Haman omitted the name of the people he sought to destroy), allowing the two men to have a conversation in which they are thinking about entirely different people. While the king is thinking of Mordecai, Haman quite naturally thinks that the king must be talking about him. After all, he knows that, outside of the king, he is the most powerful man in the empire. He has already been given the king's signet ring and has been invited to two private banquets with the king and queen. In his own mind, who else could the king possibly be talking about besides him?

Assuming that he has just been given the opportunity to prescribe his own aggrandizement, Haman suggests the highest honors he can possibly think of for this as of yet unnamed honoree. In fact, he is so full of anticipation, so beside himself with giddy excitement, that he forgets his polite address to the king. He does not begin with "if it please the king"; he just blurts out:

> For the man whom the king delights to honor, let royal robes be brought, which the king has worn, and the horse that the king has ridden, and on whose head a royal crown is set.[5] And let the robes and the horse be handed over to one of the king's most noble officials. Let them dress the man whom the king delights to honor, and let them lead him on the horse through the square of the city, proclaiming before him: "Thus shall it be done to the man whom the king delights to honor." (6:7–9)

It is hard to imagine a more indulgent suggestion. In Persia, wearing the king's robe was considered to have an almost magical aura about it, almost making one into a king.[6] It is about as close as he could get to saying, "Make the man the king!" As Adele Berlin points out,

> Haman wants to masquerade as the king; indeed, Haman wants to *be* the king. He already occupies the highest position at court (3:1), is the person to whom everyone else must bow (3:2), possesses the king's signet ring authorizing him to make edicts (3:10), and has been invited by the queen to two private dinner parties (5:12). It is but a small step to the kingship itself, and Haman now tries to take it.[7]

Of course, it is not surprising to find that Haman desires to be king. All along his actions have tended to copycat the king's. In chapter 1, Ahasuerus becomes enraged when Vashti refuses to obey a command, and he takes it out on all the women of the empire; in chapter 3, Haman becomes enraged when Mordecai refuses to obey a command, and he takes it out on all the Jews of the empire. In chapter 1, Ahasuerus is offered advice on how to deal with an insubordinate, and "this advice pleased the king"; in chapter 5, Haman is offered advice on how to deal with an insubordinate, and "this idea pleased Haman." In chapter 1, Ahasuerus rashly decides to dole out punishment overwhelmingly disproportionate to the offense done to him; in chapters 3 and 5, Haman rashly decides to dole out punishment overwhelmingly disproportionate to the offense done to him. In chapter 1, Ahasuerus impulsively vacillates between happiness and anger; in chapter 5, Haman impulsively vacillates between happiness and anger. At the beginning of chapter 5, Ahasuerus allows his wife to direct his actions; at the end of chapter 5, Haman allows his wife to direct his actions. Over and over, Ahasuerus is quick to jump to conclusions, especially ones that feed his own self-indulgence, and he has a proclivity to excess; now Haman has quickly jumped to conclusions as he excitedly feeds his own sense of self-indulgence, with a similar proclivity to excess.

In doing so, Haman has evidently forgotten why he came to the king's chamber in the middle of night. Like a child who stops a tantrum as soon as his eyes are dazzled by a piece of cake that is set down before him, Haman's impatient and enraged quest to impale Mordecai stops for the moment and his eyes become wide at the prospect of being honored by the king. After all, "honour is his life-blood, and the thought of honour will divert him even from his plan against Mordecai."[8]

However, just as quickly as Haman forgets about Mordecai, with equal quickness he is reminded of him. Upon hearing Haman's suggestion, the king responds, "That's a great idea! Let's do that! Go get *Mordecai the Jew* and do all these things for him." How shocked Haman must have felt to hear those words! But the king has ordered it, so Haman must do it. He must take the king's robe and not swing it around his own shoulders, but drape it over Mordecai's. He must take the king's horse, and instead of riding on it, he must walk in front, leading it through the streets with Mordecai mounted on it. He must herald every step of the way, "Thus shall it be done to the man whom the king delights to honor," burning inside the whole time with the thought that it should be him on top of the horse and not Mordecai. And perhaps most painfully, he must listen to the crowds in the open square cheer and acclaim Mordecai the Jew, whom he despises more than anyone else, instead of him.

How quickly things can change! The last time Mordecai's apparel was mentioned, he was wearing sackcloth and ashes; now he is wearing royal robes. The last time his posture was mentioned, he "would not rise"; now he is lifted up on the king's horse. The last time words were spoken about him, they were words plotting how the king would disgrace him; now they are words proclaiming how the king is honoring him.

Of course, the turnabout is deserved—just as Haman received the promotion that should have been Mordecai's (2:19–3:1), so now Mordecai receives the honor that Haman thinks should have been his.[9] But that never occurs to Haman. He is too bitterly crestfallen. Overcome with humiliation at having to honor his archenemy and to do so in such a public fashion, Haman hurries home with his head covered in grief. Fittingly, the three days of fasting by the Jews in Susa are just finishing; it is as if the grief has shifted from the heads of the Jews to the head of Haman.[10] Now the Jews do not have their heads covered in grief; Haman does!

Upon arriving home, he tells his wife and all his friends everything that happened to him. Immediately they sense that this cannot be by accident. This has something to do with Mordecai being Jewish. Something else is at work here, and there is no stopping it. They say, "If Mordecai, before whom you have begun to fall, is of the Jewish people, you will not overcome him but will surely fall before him" (6:13).

And they are right. Something else *is* at work. Actually, it is some*one* who is at work. We see it in all the coincidences that pile up in this relatively short period of time. It just so happens that the king cannot sleep on this particular night. It just so happens that when he calls for the royal records to be read, the attendant opens up to Mordecai's forgotten deed from five years earlier. It just so happens that Haman decides not to wait until morning, but comes to the king's court in the middle of the night and arrives at the very moment that the king is thinking about how to reward Mordecai. It just so happens that when the king asks Haman what should be done for this unnamed honoree, he neglects to mention that it is Mordecai he is talking about. So many coincidences cannot be accidental. Like a subtle signpost, they point to an invisible hand at work, orchestrating every event to accomplish a purpose. As the old adage goes, "Coincidences are just God's way of remaining anonymous." There is no mistaking it. God is at work in all these events. He is subtle; he is not expressly mentioned; but he *is* there and he *is* at work.

As a result, as bad as things began to look for Mordecai (and the Jews), God turns everything around. In fact, there is a particular point in the passage, a kind of pivot point, upon which all the events turn. Before this pivot point, Haman is joyful and glad of heart (5:9); after it, his head is covered in grief (6:12). Before it, Haman goes home to his wife and friends, who tell him he will surely prevail over Mordecai (5:10–14); after it, Haman goes home to his wife and friends, who tell him that Mordecai will surely prevail over him (6:12–13). Before it, Haman is intent on executing Mordecai (5:14); after it, Haman is forced to exalt Mordecai (6:4–11). Before it, Haman is in total control, skillfully manipulating the king at will; after it, Haman is whisked away helplessly to the banquet that Esther has prepared (6:14).

In an even wider sense, this particular pivot point is not just the turning point of the passage, but of the entire book of Esther. There are three feasts before it, and three feasts after it. There are twenty-nine mentions of Susa before it, and twenty-nine after it. Haman has the upper hand in every chapter before it, and Mordecai has the upper hand in every chapter after it. It is the point at which the whole story begins to turn around. It is the pivot point for the whole book. And, surprisingly, the pivot point is this: the king could not sleep (6:1).[11]

In fact, the entire structure of the book bears this out. The events of the book follow an ancient narrative pattern called a chiasm, which is a symmetrical arrangement in which the first event corresponds to the last event, the second event corresponds to the second-to-last event, and so on. Frequently, the center of the chiasm is of paramount importance. Significantly, in Esther, the structure is:[12]

- A. Introduction—the extent of Ahasuerus's kingdom (1:1)
  - B. Two banquets held by the king—one for the princes of all the provinces (180 days) and the other a special party for the inhabitants of Susa (7 days) (1:2–22)
    - C. Esther is taken to the king but conceals her identity (2:1–23)
      - D. Description of Haman's stature: "King Ahasuerus promotes Haman, son of Hamedatha, the Agagite, and advances him" (3:1–2)
        - E. Casting of the lot: war on the 13th of Adar (3:3–7)
          - F. Giving the ring to Haman; Haman's letters; Mordecai rending his clothes; the fast of the Jews and Esther (3:8–4:17)

G. Esther's first feast; Haman is in good spirits (5:1–8)

H. Haman's consultation with his associates and their optimism (5:9–14)

**X. The king cannot sleep and the episode of the horse (6:1–11)**

H' Haman's consultation with his associates and their pessimism (6:12–14)

G' Esther's second feast; Haman is hanged (7:1–10)

F' Giving the ring to Mordecai; Mordecai's letters; dressing of Mordecai in royal garments; feast for the Jews (8:1–17)

E' War on the 13th of Adar (9:1–2)

D' Description of the stature of the Jews and of Mordecai and their victory over their enemies: "All the princes of the provinces . . . were favoring the Jews . . . for the man Mordecai was becoming increasingly powerful" (9:3–11)

C' Esther comes before the king to request an additional day of battle in Susa, and the Gentiles "profess to be Jews" (9:12–17)

B' Two feasts for the Jews—one for the Jews of all the provinces (14th of Adar) and the other a special feast for the Jews of Susa (15th of Adar) (9:17–32)

A' Conclusion—the extent of Ahasuerus's kingdom (10:1–3)

Thus, the entire book of Esther unfolds in a strikingly symmetrical structure, in which the elements in the second half of the structure complement and largely reverse the elements in the first half of the structure. And standing at the very center of the book's structure, the pivot point on which the whole story turns, is the king's insomnia!

Such a seemingly insignificant event is hardly what might be expected as the crucial turning point. After all, Esther's realization that God has providentially placed her where she is for such a time as this would seem to be a more fitting turning point for the book. Her boldness to go to the king would also be a good candidate, as would her cleverness in arranging the two banquets. In short, the turning point of the book seems like it should come from either some great intervention by God or some admirable action on the part of a character. Instead, it comes from something as mundane and trivial as a night of insomnia. But, in the hands of God, even one night of insomnia can become a redemptive pivot point that will dramatically change the course of events.

## GOD'S PROVIDENTIAL PIVOT POINTS

The history of the world is full of events that are seemingly mundane and insignificant, but which are actually pregnant with providential meaning. Never was that more true than in the lives of people who crossed paths with Jesus. Because of the way the gospel of Matthew begins, it is easy to miss just how mundane the first encounter of Peter, Andrew, James, and John with Jesus actually was. The gospel begins with Jesus' impressive genealogy connecting him to Abraham, the father of promise, and to David, the apex of the kingdom in the Old Testament (Matt. 1:1–17); Mary's miraculous conception by the Holy Spirit (1:18–25); the supernatural guidance of the wise men from the east (2:1–12); the angelic protection of the child Jesus (2:13–23); the promise by John the Baptist that Jesus would baptize with the Holy Spirit and with fire (3:1–12);

the opening of the heavens at Jesus' own baptism and the heavenly voice's declaration that Jesus is his beloved Son (3:13–17); and the combat between Jesus and the Devil in the wilderness, in which Jesus proves victorious (4:1–11). At the end of that supernaturally saturated narrative, Jesus begins his ministry by quoting from Isaiah that a light has dawned in the darkness and that people should repent for the kingdom of heaven is at hand (4:12–17).

After such an introduction, one might expect to read next about dramatic events and powerful miracles. But what actually comes next? Matthew tells us:

> While [Jesus was] walking by the Sea of Galilee, he saw two brothers, Simon (who is called Peter) and Andrew his brother, casting a net into the sea, for they were fishermen. And he said to them, "Follow me, and I will make you fishers of men." (4:18–19)

Of course, there is no indication that these four fishermen are aware at this point of everything that Matthew has made his readers aware of. They are simply casting their nets into the sea, going about their daily work to provide for their needs. There was no indication that this day would be any different from the thousands of other days on which they went out to cast their nets into the Sea of Galilee. But this is not a normal day. While they are working, Jesus issues them a call. He does not dress it up. He does not accompany it with demonstrations of power. He simply calls them to follow him. And in a moment they decide to do just that. They leave their nets and follow him.

Similarly, Jesus sees another pair of brothers, this time James and John, the sons of Zebedee. To them too he issues a call, and they too drop what they're doing and follow him. With their father still in the boat, they decide to follow this man (4:21–22). One could not imagine a moment that would change their lives more than that one. Everything would be different from now on. Their lives would be different, their experiences would be different, and, most importantly, they would be different. And all happened because on a normal day, while doing normal things, a man named Jesus passed by them and called them to join him, and they decided in that moment to follow him.

So too with a tax collector named Zacchaeus. Jesus happened to be passing through the town of Jericho, and for whatever reason the interest (no pun intended) of this chief tax collector was piqued. In the gospel of Luke, we read that Zacchaeus makes his way into the crowd to see Jesus. However, because the crowd is large and Zacchaeus is short, there is no way he can see Jesus. So he runs on ahead and climbs up into a sycamore tree to get a better view. When Jesus comes by, he looks up in the tree, notices Zacchaeus, and tells him to come down, so that they can go to his house and eat together. That single event radically changes this tax collector's life forever. His heart now full of joy and melted by Jesus' gracious welcome, Zacchaeus dedicates half his goods to the poor and promises to restore fourfold all the money he has unjustly taken from people (Luke 19:1–10). Of course, Luke does not reveal what Zacchaeus's state of mind was earlier in the day, but it is not unreasonable to assume that this day began like most other days, with Zacchaeus doing normal things on a normal day. However, the simple and seemingly insignificant events of climbing up in a sycamore tree and having a meal with Jesus set his life on a new course forever. Just as with the four fishermen at the beginning of Jesus' ministry, seemingly mundane events become in God's providential hands the pivot points for something truly significant.

But the greatest pivot point was on Good Friday and Easter Sunday. As with the plight of the Jews in Esther's day, things went downhill dramatically, swiftly, and despairingly. Less than one week before, Jesus had ridden into Jerusalem on a donkey and crowds had spread their cloaks and leafy branches across the road, heralding him as the one who had come to make God's kingdom a reality. But now everything had changed. Like Mordecai, Jesus was now facing an unjust death on a wooden stake, as if he were merely a common criminal. And yet what seemed to so many at the time as a hopeless, meaningless, incomprehensible, and tragic event—an execution on a common Roman cross on the outskirts of the empire—was in the providential hands of God the hinge of history, the redemptive pivot point for the whole world.

As a result, his followers in the book of Acts begin to preach and teach boldly about the good news that Jesus has died on the cross for our sins and been raised from the dead so that we might have new life. However, just as Haman became infuriated at Mordecai, so now the high priest becomes infuriated with the apostles. He arrests them and puts them in prison. In the middle of the night, an angel opens the prison door and sets them free. The next day they enter the temple and begin to teach once again. Perplexed, the high priest asks them why they continue to teach. In response, Peter and the apostles answer,

> We must obey God rather than men. The God of our fathers raised Jesus, whom you killed by hanging him on a tree. God exalted him at his right hand as Leader and Savior, to give repentance to Israel and forgiveness of sins. And we are witnesses to these things, and so is the Holy Spirit, whom God has given to those who obey him. (Acts 5:29–32)

Just as Haman did with Mordecai, the high priest becomes infuriated a second time with the apostles and, along with the rest of the council, wants to kill them. But a Pharisee in the council named Gamaliel, who is a teacher of the law and highly esteemed, rises up to counsel them with words that are eerily similar to Zeresh's counsel to Haman. He says,

> Men of Israel, take care what you are about to do with these men. For before these days Theudas rose up, claiming to be somebody, and a number of men, about four hundred, joined him. He was killed, and all who followed him were dispersed and came to nothing. After him Judas the Galilean rose up in the days of the census and drew away some of the people after him. He too perished, and all who followed him were scattered. So in the present case I tell you, keep away from these men and let them alone, for if this plan or this undertaking is of man, it will fail; but if it is of God, you will not be able to overthrow them. You might even be found opposing God! (Acts 5:35–39)

Taking his advice, the council members decide not to put them to death, but instead to beat them and charge them not to continue teaching. This the apostles promptly ignore. They enter the temple and go from house to house every day, teaching and preaching that Jesus is the Messiah.

Perhaps, at this point, the reader would expect something supernatural to validate and support the apostles' ministry. Instead, we get another rather mundane situation. Some of the Greek-speaking widows feel that they are being neglected in the daily distribution of food (probably not intentionally, but just because of poor administration). Not wanting this to continue, the apostles summon the full number of disciples and set aside seven men who have good reputations and appoint them to remedy the situation (Acts 6:1–6). Again, the normal distribution of food among widows might seem to be something mundane, not nearly of the same importance as the preaching and teaching ministry of the apostles. But nothing could be further from the truth. Their ministry becomes a vital part of God's work to multiply the number of disciples in Jerusalem and to draw a great many priests to the faith (Acts 6:7).

As a result, Christians should take heart. Whether it is with the seemingly normal day of fishing on the Sea of

Galilee for Peter, Andrew, James, and John, the seemingly ordinary affairs of tax collecting in Jericho for Zacchaeus, or the seemingly mundane issue of distributing food in Jerusalem, the seemingly insignificant and ordinary events in life can be used by God to effect a turn in people's lives. In fact, it is often through such seemingly mundane and insignificant events that the Lord's invisible hands are at work, carrying out his purposes in the most subtle of ways.

The same thing is true today. Looking back over your life, you will surely see all kinds of seemingly mundane or insignificant events that became life-changing pivot points—that phone call out of the blue, that chance meeting that you never saw coming, that off-the-cuff comment someone made, that decision that at the time seemed to have no particularly great importance. At the time, they may have seemed insignificant, and yet they became very significant and powerfully redemptive. They were God's anonymous moments, moments that he used to change your life forever.

So, too, there are all kinds of events that are happening in our lives in the present, which look pointless, meaningless, and insignificant. Of course, many of them may in fact have no "appreciable" effect on the future. But within the constant stream of circumstances, situations, and events that make up our lives, there are little things happening, little turns of events, little details that God is invisibly orchestrating with his hands, so that they form redemptive pivot points in our lives—even if we don't see it happening and can't see it happening. In one of his memoirs, the Presbyterian pastor Frederick Buechner wrote, "There is no event so commonplace but that God is present within it, always leaving you room to recognize him or not to recognize him, but all the more fascinatingly because of that, all the more compellingly and hauntingly."[13]

And to acknowledge that simple but profound reality means that the details of our lives have a greater depth than we can possibly fathom, a greater significance than we could ever hope for, and a greater importance than we can even imagine. To appreciate that is to live differently. Every day becomes a walk of faith. Every day, regardless of what it holds, becomes an opportunity for God to work. Every day is filled with potential "divine appointments." Who knows what moments today will be pivotal in your life? Who knows what God might be ordaining through a phone call or email that you receive? Who knows what circumstances God is lining up in your life that you cannot see right now? Who knows what decisions will become hinges in his providential hands? And who knows—as hard as it can sometimes be to accept it—what disappointments, closed doors, and trying situations God might be using in his ever-so-subtle way to work out his plan in your life?

The truth is that there are no coincidences in the world or happenstances in our lives. Everything that happens is under the superintendence of our sovereign God, who subtly and providentially works out his purposes, even through seemingly insignificant events like a Persian king's insomnia or a Galilean fisherman's call or a common Roman cross. As the nineteenth-century Anglican bishop J. C. Ryle once said,

> There is no such thing as "chance," "luck" or "accident" in the Christian's journey through this world. All is arranged and appointed by God. . . . [Therefore] let us seek to have an abiding sense of God's hand in all that befalls us, if we profess to be believers in Jesus Christ. Let us strive to realize that a Father's hand is measuring out our daily portion, and that our steps are ordered by Him.[14]

## FOR FURTHER REFLECTION

1. What are some key events in your life that looked insignificant at the time but proved to be determinative?

2. How can the perspective that God providentially orchestrates his purposes through many seemingly insignificant events in our lives change the way we look at the "normal" and "regular" parts of our day-to-day lives?
3. What does it mean to live with the confidence that God is ordering all of our steps?

CHAPTER EIGHT

# POETIC JUSTICE (7:1–10)

*If there is not an over-ruling Providence ordering all things for the good of God's people, how comes it to pass that the good and evil which is done to them in this world is accordingly repaid into the bosoms of them that are instrumental therein? (John Flavel*[1]*)*

Time has seemed to move considerably slower in the middle part of the book. The events in chapters 1–2 stretch over the course of several years, but the events since chapter 3 stretch over the course of only a few days. On this particular day, the king wakes up during the night and cannot get back to sleep. A little later, Haman arrives at the palace to seek the king's permission to hang Mordecai. However, through a comedy of errors, Haman must honor his archenemy Mordecai. Sometime in the morning, Haman robes Mordecai and leads him through the square of the city to be honored. Afterward, he scurries home in disgrace. Soon after that, the eunuchs arrive and whisk him away to the second banquet that Esther has prepared for him and the king.

## ESTHER MAKES HER REQUEST (7:1–6)

Although the narrator does not reveal Haman's inner thoughts at this point, perhaps Haman, in his irrepressible pride, thinks that his luck is about to change. Even though the morning was humiliating, at least now he gets to go to the private and exclusive dinner with the royal couple. Perhaps things will go better for him from now on. After all, at virtually every turn in the story, Haman's primary motivation is not so much ethnic hatred, though he certainly has that. Nor is it monetary gain, though he certainly is wealthy. At every step, Haman is primarily driven by a need to confirm his power. He has revealed himself to be a man desperately in need of being in control and having others come under his authority. Each time he becomes enraged at Mordecai, it is because of Mordecai's refusal to recognize his position. Even all his wealth, his many sons, and his public honors cannot take away the sting of these slights. Conversely, the only times in the book when Haman seems happy is when his ego is being stroked. When he gets the invitation to Esther's second banquet, he walks out of the first banquet filled with joy and merriment. When he comes to the palace in the middle of the night and believes the king is about to shower him with honor, he can hardly contain his giddy excitement. When his power is publicly compromised, his wounded ego must repair itself by boasting to his wife and friends about all the ways that he really is powerful, important, and significant. So, perhaps now, Haman is consoling himself with his own greatness for being included in such an exclusive feast.

The world has always had its Hamans. There have always been people with an almost insatiable lust for control and power and an incessant need for other people to show them respect. They will do whatever they have to do to get it—and, once they have it, to keep it. Like Haman, they have no scruples about manipulating things to further their self-serving agenda. They traffic in deception without any conviction in their conscience. If other people get in the way, or if they perceive that someone else is a threat, they do whatever they have to do to get rid of them. They live within their own narcissistic world and refuse to see beyond their own self-interests. They show a startling level of insensitivity toward other people, for they are not really that concerned about others; they are concerned only about themselves. Without a second thought, they trample on others if it helps them to get power or keep it. Without the slightest remorse, they abuse or even destroy others, if it furthers their agenda.

Within history, the pattern has been played out countless times. In the twentieth century alone, Adolf Hitler had a never-satiated ego that wanted to conquer the whole world, and, like Haman, he thought nothing of trying to wipe out the whole Jewish population in the process. As the ruling power in Haiti for nearly three decades, the Duvalier family fostered a personality cult and lavish lifestyles to aggrandize themselves, while at the same time using force and corruption to slaughter nearly 30,000 Haitians and to plunge the rest of the people into poverty virtually unrivaled in the Western world. Similarly, in North Korea, the ruling Kim family has also insisted on a personality cult that includes deification and has accumulated massive wealth and power, while much of the country lives in squalor. Anyone not showing the proper reverence toward their Supreme Leader receives swift punishment, whether in the form of hard labor or execution. The examples quickly multiply—Idi Amin in Uganda, Benito Mussolini in Italy, Pol Pot in Cambodia, Joseph Stalin in Russia, Théoneste Bagosora in Rwanda, Mao Zedong in China, Saddam Hussein in Iraq, and Rafael Trujillo in the Dominican Republic. Each of them, like Haman, had an unquenchable thirst for power and an unrelenting brutality toward anyone who threatened it.

Haman stands as the prototype for all the mass murderers, tyrannical despots, and ruthless dictators. But now he comes to his day of reckoning. Having arrived at the banquet that Esther has prepared, Haman sits down with the king and queen to eat and drink just as they had all done the day before. While they are drinking, the king turns to Esther and asks her once again, "What is your wish, Queen Esther? It shall be granted you. And what is your request? Even to the half of my kingdom, it shall be fulfilled" (7:2).

This time Esther does not defer the issue or skirt the question. As will become clear, Haman is not the only one in the royal palace who knows how to manipulate the king with shrewdness of speech. She begins, "If I have found favor in your sight, O king, and if it please the king . . ." (v. 3). That is a very clever way to begin. Her opening address is slightly different from her previous addresses in the book. Previously, she referred to the king only in the third person when making her requests—"If it please the king, let the king . . ." (5:4, 8). But now she subtly changes her address to the king to be in the second person—"If I have found favor in *your* sight, O king." By doing so, Esther delicately emphasizes her close relationship to him. Even in her address, she is using her words to pull herself close to him.

Then she continues by pulling her people close to herself. She says, "Let my life be granted me for my wish, and my people for my request" (v. 3). That is a subtle shift from the king's question. His question implied that the "request" and the "petition" referred to one desire of Esther. But she capitalizes on the fact that he has used two synonyms and makes two requests, not one. She petitions him for her own life, and requests from him her people's life. She is lumping together her destiny and the destiny of her people. They are one and the same to her. In this way, she begins to pull together the king, Esther herself, and the concern she has for her people.

She continues, "For we have been sold, I and my people, to be destroyed, to be killed, and to be annihilated" (v. 4). In stating that she and her people have been sold, Esther is subtly suggesting that a gravely treasonous act has been perpetrated against the king. After all, within an empire, who has the right to sell a whole people group? The king and only the king! To imply that someone else has stepped in and begun selling away part of the kingdom is to suggest that someone else is trying to wrest power away from the king. In other words, there's a traitor in your kingdom! This, of course, occurs on the very same day that the king had been reminded of how someone thwarted a plot against him. Now Esther is presenting herself as the one who is uncovering for him another plot, this time against both the king and the queen.

The plot itself, she says, is for her and her people to be destroyed, killed, and annihilated. Apparently, the king does not realize that these are the same three words that were used in Haman's edict. Nevertheless, Esther has cunningly laid the trap for Haman. She has cleverly and slyly used the very words of his edict in such a way that it will inevitably be seen, not only as a threat against the queen, but also as a traitorous act against the king himself.

Finally, she finishes with a brilliant piece of rhetoric: "If we had merely been sold as male and female slaves, I would have kept quiet, because no such distress would justify disturbing the king" (v. 4 NIV). This is especially shrewd for two different reasons. On merely a surface level, this statement curries favor with the king. By telling him that she would have kept quiet if she and her people had merely been sold as slaves, because she would not want to disturb him, she implies that she is at least as concerned about the king's peace of mind as she is about her own life. To a king who has shown repeatedly that he does not like to be disturbed or bothered, this can only ingratiate the queen even more with him.

But, at a deeper level, she is subtly establishing yet another connection with Haman's edict, which will become evident to the king only as the events play out. When Haman came to the king to sell (quite literally) the idea of exterminating an entire people group, he said, "There is a certain people scattered abroad and dispersed among the peoples in all the provinces of your kingdom.

Their laws are different from those of every other people, and they do not keep the king's laws, so that it is not to the king's profit to tolerate them. If it please the king, let it be decreed that they be destroyed, and I will pay 10,000 talents of silver into the hands of those who have charge of the king's business, that they may put it into the king's treasuries" (3:8–9). The key part is in verse 9. Haman requests a decree that this people be destroyed, and he will pay an enormous sum of silver as compensation. However, in the Hebrew, the word for "destroy" (*'bd*) is a homophone of the word for "enslave" (*'bd*).[2] That is, they sound the same, even though their meanings are different. What appears to have happened, then, is that Haman solicited the king's permission to kill the Jews, but did so with an ambiguous word, such that when he followed the request with a payment of money, the king would naturally but mistakenly think that Haman was requesting merely to enslave a group of people. If that, indeed, is what happened (and it would certainly explain why Ahasuerus seems to be completely unaware and surprised that there is a plot to destroy a whole people group), then Esther's shrewd concluding statement will both let the king off the hook and further close the trap on Haman when everything comes to light in the following moments. That is, once she reveals to the king who it is that has done this dastardly thing, the king will not only be able to save face in the matter of the plot, but his fury toward Haman will be compounded because it will be obvious that Haman has not only threatened the queen, but also tricked the king in order to do it. All in all, Esther's phrasing shows brilliant rhetorical skill.

Not surprisingly, the king immediately becomes white-hot with rage, as he has done so many times before. "Who is he, and where is he, who has dared to do this?" he demands to know (v. 5). In Hebrew, the king's question begins with six monosyllabic words, "which sound like machine-gun fire when pronounced aloud."[3]

Then, with perfect timing, Esther drops the hammer. With her staccato response, her words almost convey the sense of a verbal finger-pointing as she thunders out with perfect cadence, "A foe and enemy! This wicked Haman!" (v. 6). Immediately terror strikes Haman. In describing it, the narrator paints a powerful picture with an economy of words: "Then Haman was terrified before the king and the queen" (v. 6). The phrasing clearly portrays Haman on one side and the king and queen united against him. Not only that, but the narrator does not refer to Ahasuerus and Esther by their names (as he does in the earlier part of the verse), but by their titles, which emphasizes the relationship they have to one another. She is not Esther here; she is the queen, the royal woman who is married to the king. Now exposed and standing before them all alone, Haman is speechless and terrified.

## HAMAN IS HANGED (7:7–10)

The king, for his part, is so enraged that he storms out of the room and retreats to the palace garden, momentarily at a loss as to what to do with this new information. His right-hand man—a traitor and an assassin! Haman, realizing that the king will mete out severe punishment when he returns, stays in the banquet hall, falls down before the queen, and pleads with her for his life. A few moments earlier, it was Esther who was pleading for her life; now it is Haman who is doing the pleading! The poetic justice is exquisite: the man who became so enraged at a Jew for refusing to bow before him that he wanted to take the Jew's life is now reduced to groveling before a Jew to beg for his own life.

The king returns to the banquet hall and sees Haman falling on the couch where Esther is. Of course, Haman is only begging for his life, but to the king it looks like something else entirely.[4] In Persian culture, no one but the king was allowed within seven steps of the wife or concubine of the king.[5] But here is Haman, falling down upon the queen's couch. Haman, the man who had taken the king's signet ring and tried to take the king's robe and horse, now appears to the king as if he is trying to take his wife too!

Significantly, the narrator does not use the word "bow down" here, even though that would have been the more natural word choice. Instead, he uses the word "fall," for this truly is Haman's fall, the irony of which should not go unappreciated.[6] When Haman initially plotted the destruction of the Jews, he caused the lot to "fall" (3:7; the word "fall" does not appear in the English translation, but the Hebrew word is the same). When the king instructed Haman to honor Mordecai in the city square, he told him (literally), "Do not let fall anything that you have said" (6:10; again, the word "fall" does not appear in the English, but is the same word in the Hebrew). Then, when Haman rushed home, his wife forecasted that he was already beginning to fall before Mordecai (6:13). Now Haman does indeed fall—before the queen and, quickly enough, at the hand of the king as well.

Seeing Haman fall onto the couch where the queen is, the king exclaims, "Will he even assault the queen in my presence, in my own house?" (v. 8). The word for "assault" (*kbsh*) has the sense of "subdue" or "subjugate by force," and here it indicates sexual assault or rape. The king, quite naturally, is outraged. Nevertheless, the irony is that the same king who cared so little for the sexual propriety and honor of the queen in chapter 1 suddenly cares so much about the sexual propriety and honor of the queen now.[7] But the inconsistency of the king brings about just deserts for Haman: the man who has manipulated the king with misunderstandings is now being done in by another one of the king's misunderstandings. He has falsely accused the Jews of treason against the king, and now he is falsely accused of treason against the king.

Again, Haman is speechless—not that he has much of a chance to say anything. Without delay, they (presumably the eunuchs who are the king's attendants) cover Haman's face. Elsewhere in Scripture, covering one's face is an image of grief or shame (cf. 2 Sam. 19:4; Pss. 44:15; 69:7; Jer. 51:51). That is why, earlier in the day, after Haman was forced to honor Mordecai in the city square, he hurried home with his head covered in disgrace (6:12). But now the second most powerful man in the empire is rendered completely powerless. He does not cover his own head; others come and cover it for him.

Then, as if on cue, one of the king's eunuchs, Harbona, steps forward and says, "Moreover, the gallows that Haman has prepared for Mordecai, whose word saved the king, is standing at Haman's house, fifty cubits high" (v. 9). As of yet, the king has not pronounced a death sentence, but the eunuch makes it none too difficult to connect the dots with his timely suggestion. The appeal to the king is clear. Issuing his first direct command in the book, he says, "Hang him on that" (v. 10).

Immediately they take Haman back to his own house and execute him on the gallows, just as had been done to the traitors previously exposed by Mordecai (2:23). How ironic it is that the man who was seated high above everyone else (3:1) is now hanged high above everyone else.[8] The man who has been so obsessed with his own elevation is now truly elevated—fifty cubits high! Here is the perfect and proportional reversal: Haman is hanged on the very gallows that he prepared for Mordecai, and the very disgrace and public humiliation that he designed for Mordecai now becomes his own final fate. Mordecai has gotten the honor that Haman wanted for himself, and Haman has gotten the gallows that he wanted for Mordecai.

Oh, how the mighty has fallen—and how swiftly! At the beginning of the day, Haman was on top of the world, with power, wealth, and honor. By the end of the day, he has fallen into utter humiliation and disgrace. The day began with him coming to the palace to seek Mordecai's execution, but the day ends with him being led away from the palace to endure his own execution. And there is such poetic justice. Haman gets exactly what he deserves in the exact measure that he deserves it. He is like the man described in the Psalms:

> Behold, the wicked man conceives evil
>     and is pregnant with mischief
>     and gives birth to lies.
> He makes a pit, digging it out,
>     and falls into the hole that he has made.
> His mischief returns upon his own head,
>     and on his own skull his violence descends.
>         (Ps. 7:14–16; cf. Prov. 26:27; 28:10)

And that is one of the chief purposes for God's providence in this world—to set things right in the end, and to do it with perfect justice and exact measure.

## THE PROVIDENCE OF GOD AND THE DESTINY OF THE WICKED

The truth is, there is something deeply satisfying about the maker of an evil plan falling victim to his own evil designs. In Shakespeare's *Hamlet*, prince Hamlet is seeking to avenge the murder of his father. A ghost has revealed to him that Hamlet's uncle poured poison into the late king's ear, causing him to perish. At one point in the story, the uncle (and now king), Claudius, sends two men, Rosencrantz and Guildenstern, to check on Hamlet. Initially, Hamlet greets them warmly, but he quickly realizes that they have come not in friendship, but as spies. Now the wiser, Hamlet is suspicious when Claudius sends the two men with him to England. Finding a letter from

Claudius to the king of England instructing him to have Hamlet put to death, Hamlet changes the letter so that it instructs the king to put Rosencrantz and Guildenstern, his betrayers, to death instead. In speaking of the poetic justice, Hamlet says,

> There's letters seal'd: and my two schoolfellows,
> Whom I will trust as I will adders fang'd,
> They bear the mandate; they must sweep my way
> And marshal me to knavery. Let it work;
> For 'tis the sport to have the enginer
> Hoist with his own petar ; and 't shall go hard
> But I will delve one yard below their mines
> And blow them at the moon: O, 'tis most sweet,
> When in one line two crafts directly meet.[9]

In the end, the corrupt king, Claudius, meets a similar fate. Hamlet stabs him and then forces the king to drink from his own poisoned cup.

Just as Hamlet took a certain delight in seeing his betrayers "hoist with their own petards" and the king "drink from his own cup," so there is a certain delight in seeing Haman hung on his own gallows. The delight comes, not from *Schadenfreude* (meaning "pleasure in someone else's misery or misfortune"), but from a deep longing for justice and a yearning for evil to be overturned and for things in the world to be set right.

In that sense, Haman's downfall is a manifestation of God's providential work in the world to overturn evil with a sense of poetic justice, a work that begins its climactic realization in the birth of Jesus. In the gospel of Luke, when Mary has become pregnant, she breaks out in song. Mary magnifies the Lord for his gracious treatment of her. Using various passages from the Old Testament, she offers up a beautiful song celebrating a redemptive reversal that has the powers of this world being brought low and the humble being raised up. She sings:

> He has shown strength with his arm;
> he has scattered the proud in the thoughts of their hearts;
> he has brought down the mighty from their thrones
> and exalted those of humble estate;
> he has filled the hungry with good things,
> and the rich he has sent away empty.
> (Luke 1:51–53)

Throughout his ministry, Jesus consistently embodied this reversal in his ministry. The strong he brought down with his messianic power, announcing that he had come to bind the strong man (Satan) and to break his hold on the world (Matt. 12:22–32; cf. Luke 10:17–20). The proud he brought low with his preaching, pronouncing woes on the scribes and the Pharisees (Matt. 23:1–36). The powerful he brought down with his indictments, proclaiming judgment on the Sadducees and the temple hierarchy (Matt. 24:1–35). By contrast, the poor he blessed, the outcast he restored, the marginalized he helped, the diseased he cured, the oppressed he freed, the crippled he healed, the hungry he fed, and the despised he loved.

In Luke's version of the Beatitudes, Jesus makes this reversal explicit as he describes how the kingdom of God turns the values and powers of this world on their head:

> Blessed are you who are poor, for yours is the kingdom of God.
>
> Blessed are you who are hungry now, for you shall be satisfied.
>
> Blessed are you who weep now, for you shall laugh.
>
> Blessed are you when people hate you and when they exclude you and revile you and spurn your name as evil, on account of the Son of Man! Rejoice in that day, and leap for joy, for behold, your reward

> is great in heaven; for so their fathers did to the prophets.
>
> But woe to you who are rich, for you have received your consolation.
>
> Woe to you who are full now, for you shall be hungry.
>
> Woe to you who laugh now, for you shall mourn and weep.
>
> Woe to you, when all people speak well of you, for so their fathers did to the false prophets. (Luke 6:20–26)

But, in some sense, Jesus' entire ministry of bringing down the mighty and lifting up the lowly was a dramatic anticipation of the ultimate reversal in history—his crucifixion and resurrection. At Calvary, it looked as if the architect of evil himself may have orchestrated the execution of God's own Son, much as Haman had been the architect of Mordecai's execution. By all appearances, evil won the battle. Yet what appeared to be a rousing victory on the part of Satan and the forces of evil, ended up being the petard on which he was hoisted. On the cross, Jesus assumed our sin, took the blows from evil, and entered into our death. But in doing so, he exhausted the penalty for sin, triumphed over evil, and conquered death. That is, sin was skewered by its own sinfulness. Evil was defeated by its own evil designs. Death was, in the words of John Owen, put to death in the death of Christ.[10]

In a memorable sermon, St. Augustine preached,

> The devil was defeated by his own victorious achievement. . . . The devil was exultant when Christ died, and by that very death of Christ was the devil conquered; it's as though he took the bait in a mousetrap. He was delighted at the death, as being the commander of death; what he delighted in, that's where the trap was set for him. The mousetrap for the devil was the cross of the Lord; the bait he would

> be caught by, the death of the Lord. And our Lord Jesus Christ rose again. Where now is the death that hung on the cross?[11]

Or, to use the words of the author of Hebrews,

> Since therefore the children share in flesh and blood, [Jesus] himself likewise partook of the same things, that through death he might destroy the one who has the power of death, that is, the devil, and deliver all those who through fear of death were subject to lifelong slavery. (Heb. 2:14–15)

In other words, what appeared to be the instrument of Satan's victory turned out, ironically and poetically, to be the very instrument of his defeat. And if Satan has been defeated by the cross and the resurrection, then such will be the fate of all the Hamans of the world. Their lies, manipulation, pride, and cruelty will not go unchecked. Injustice will not prevail forever. No, the death and resurrection of Christ announce loud and clear that their time is up and that one day their mouths will be closed. One day their pride will be stopped. One day they will be called to account, and their cruelty will finally come to an end with perfect, measured justice.

Such an end is powerfully portrayed in John's description of Babylon's downfall in Revelation. In the first century, Babylon was the iconic epitome of the cruel and proud tyranny of Rome. In John's vision, however, an angel comes down from heaven having great authority, and the earth is made bright with his glory. Calling out with a mighty voice, he announces,

> Fallen, fallen is Babylon the great!
> . . . . . . . . . . . . . . . . . . . . . .
> Pay her back as she herself has paid back others,
> and repay her double for her deeds;

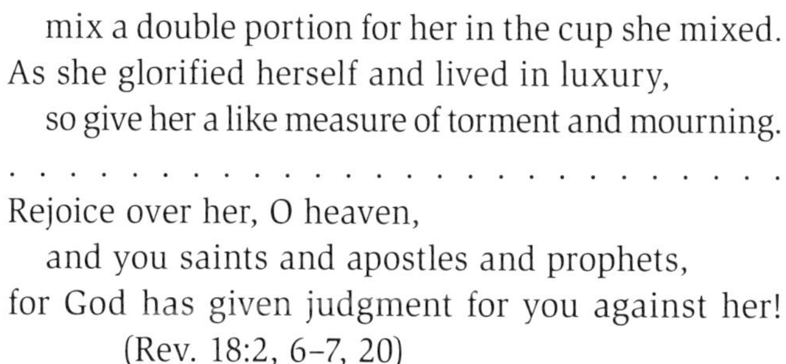

mix a double portion for her in the cup she mixed.
As she glorified herself and lived in luxury,
so give her a like measure of torment and mourning.

. . . . . . . . . . . . . . . . . . . . . . . . . . .

Rejoice over her, O heaven,
and you saints and apostles and prophets,
for God has given judgment for you against her!
(Rev. 18:2, 6–7, 20)

To Haman the gallows, to Rosencrantz and Guildenstern the petard, to Satan the cross, and to Babylon the cup—poetic justice will eventually come in the end. Such will be the fate of all the Hamans of the world. Their power seems to be unstoppable, but it will ultimately become their own downfall. Their cruelty seems to be unrestrained, but it will ultimately become their own undoing. Their self-aggrandizement seems to be unchecked, but it will ultimately become their own humiliation.

As a result, Christians today should delight in the eventual downfall of evil, just as the Jews in Esther's day no doubt delighted in the impaling of Haman or Hamlet delighted in the slaying of his betrayers. As Barry Webb writes,

> [Esther] invites us . . . to rejoice in [Haman's] downfall. Haman is not us, but our enemy. He embodies, in a most striking way, that inveterate hatred that the world has always had, and always will have, for God's people (John 17:14). And his downfall is not our achievement, but God's—a gift to be marveled at and rejoiced in. As part of its total message, the Bible's laughter is an anticipation of the eschaton; a reminder of the fact that, in a world where God remains sovereign, it is not the proud and cruel who will have the last laugh, but God and his people (Rev. 18:20).[12]

Therefore, as Christians continue to live in a world filled with mass murderers, tyrannical despots, and ruthless dictators, as Christians tend to struggle as God's people in a world that so often hates them and seeks to destroy them, whether in body or in spirit, we must commit ourselves to an attitude of unfailing trust in God and his inscrutable workings. As the Puritan Thomas Brooks once said,

> The wheels in a watch or in a clock move contrary one to another—some one way, some another; yet all show the skill and intent of the workman, to show the time, or to make the clock to strike; so in this world divine providences seem to run cross to divine promises, the wicked are spared, and the righteous are taken away; yet, in the conclusion, all issues in the will, purpose, and glory of God.[13]

We must have faith that God's providential work is under way, and that he is ordering things according to his purposes. Despite appearances in the present, we must trust that, in the conclusion of all things, the Hamans of the world will be hung on their gallows. There is some comfort in knowing that. So often, the perpetrators of evil in our world seem to get away scot-free, without any apparent consequences for their actions. But the downfall of Haman and its greater fulfillment in the defeat of Satan at Calvary must engender trust in us that God holds the world's scales in his hand and that he has promised us that he will balance them in due time.

Related to that, Christians must show persevering patience. Waiting for justice while the Hamans and Hitlers and Husseins do their evil work can stretch our patience to its breaking point. Like the martyrs in Revelation who have been the victims of such cruelty and injustice, we too want to cry out, "O Sovereign Lord, . . . how long before you will judge?" (Rev. 6:10). We must remember that it may be a long time in coming, but God's justice never fails.

Eventually his justice will come to fruition and evil will reap what it has sown, in perfect and exact measure. The perpetrators of evil may get away with their actions for a season, but one day they will meet their own gallows, be hoisted on their own petards, and drink their own cups. Christians must learn to persevere in the meantime, as God works in his providence, just as he did to Haman, to orchestrate their fall and their ultimate judgment.

Finally, in the meantime, Christians must "live consciously out of tune with the world as it presently is and in tune with the way God intends it to be."[14] To do that, Christians should be people of prayer, people who pray assiduously for justice to come and for God to make things right. Christians should be people who take up the cries for justice, the frustrations of injustice, and the desires for the latter to become the former, into heartfelt prayers that long for a world afflicted by evil to be healed by the justice of God. And, of course, in praying for justice to come on earth as it is in heaven, we also become agents and mediums through which God brings his work to bear in our lives and in the world in which we live. That is, as we take before him the cries against injustice, we become changed in the process, so that our lives increasingly become heralds of the glorious truth that evil's time is almost up. Our lives become proleptic embodiments of what the world will look like when God sets everything right—lives that are pictures of justice, lives that stand up against evil in all its forms and announce to mass murderers, tyrannical despots, and ruthless dictators that they will be called to account for their actions.

In sum, we should take heart, for God assures us that there will be final justice for all the Hamans in our world. In the end, they will not have the last word. Their lies and manipulation will not go unchecked. Neither will their obsession with control and their insatiable need for power, nor their pride or their cruelty. They may get away with it for a time, but eventually they will receive their just deserts. They will hang on their own gallows. Then the Lord will say, "My providence has run its course. My purposes are complete. My justice is established." And then all those in Christ will call back to him, along with the roar of the great multitudes in heaven, "Hallelujah! Salvation and glory and power belong to our God, for his judgments are true and just" (Rev. 19:1–2).

## FOR FURTHER REFLECTION

1. What is the difference between delighting in the truth that God will eventually establish his justice and delighting in someone's misfortune? How can we do the first without falling into the second?
2. What injustices in the world or in your own life are you eager to see God reverse?
3. What makes it hard to wait in the meantime? What can make it easier?

CHAPTER NINE

# THE TABLES ARE TURNED (8:1–9:19)

*It is the living God of history who bends and breaks His challengers, who makes an end to wars and directs the wars of the Lord, and who as the Holy One is active in all the world, spanning the length and breadth of it. In no phase of the world's history is the rule of God in danger. (G. C. Berkouwer[1])*

Haman's downfall and execution are cause for celebration, for he has gotten his just deserts. He has hung on the gallows he prepared for Mordecai, and justice has been served. But the crisis is far from over. "Haman is dead, but his edict lives on."[2] In about eleven months, the Jews in the Persian Empire will still face extermination. Fortunately, God's providence continues to orchestrate a solution.

After Haman is executed on the gallows, the king's anger abates for the second time in the book (7:10; cf. 2:1). In both instances, the abating of his anger is part of a larger pattern. In the first instance, the king becomes upset with Vashti and gets rid of her, his anger is abated, and then he finds and installs a replacement queen. Now, following the same pattern, the king becomes upset with Haman, and gets rid of him, his anger is abated, and he must now find and install a replacement official.[3]

## ESTHER AND MORDECAI'S COUNTER-EDICT (8:1–17)

Fortunately, there is a man ready at hand who makes a perfect candidate. Since Haman has been exposed as a traitor against the royal couple, his entire estate reverts back to the crown, as was the custom in Achaemenid Persia. For someone as powerful as Haman, the estate would have been considerable, likely consisting of land, property, buildings, money, servants, and even his family members.[4]

Having such a large estate now at his disposal, Ahasuerus must decide what to do with it. In one of the only decisions the king actually makes by himself, he chooses to give it to Esther, presumably because it serves a sense of justice to give to the victim what formerly belonged to the victimizer. Then, when Mordecai comes into the presence of the king, the king gives him the signet ring that once belonged to Haman, and Esther puts him in charge of Haman's estate. Just as Haman received the lot he designed for Mordecai, so now Mordecai ends up with the lot in life of Haman!

Actually, this is merely the first of many reversals. The next one comes when Esther pleads once again with the king. She falls at his feet, weeps before him, and pleads with him to avert the evil plan that Haman set in motion against the Jews. Since emotional genuflection and tears introduce an unwelcome awkwardness at the court, Esther's display of great emotion cannot be for mere effect; she must truly be distraught.[5]

Once again, the king extends his golden scepter, indicating Esther's favorable reception by the king. However, Esther does not need to defer her request with banquet invitations, as she did before. She has proven herself intensely loyal to Ahasuerus and, without Haman around to outwit, she is free to leverage her current favor to convince the king to revoke Haman's genocidal edict. So Esther stands before him and says,

> If it please the king, and if I have found favor in his sight, and if the thing seems right before the king, and I am pleasing in his eyes, let an order be written to revoke the letters devised by Haman the Agagite, the son of Hammedatha, which he wrote to destroy the Jews who are in all the provinces of the king. For how can I bear to see the calamity that is coming to my people? Or how can I bear to see the destruction of my kindred? (8:5–6)

Even now, when Esther has gained the upper hand, she still displays her superior rhetorical skill. She begins by piling up deferential clauses at the beginning, four to be exact, and alternating between the abstract and the personal. In the first and third clauses, she emphasizes the condition that the request itself will find the king's favor, while in the second and fourth clauses, she emphasizes the condition that she herself will find the king's favor. By alternating back and forth, she braids together the king's favor toward her, which is clearly high at the moment, and the king's favor toward her (as yet unarticulated) request. Only then does she set forth her request, asking that the previous edict be revoked. When she does make her request, she quite shrewdly refers to the previous edict as the letters devised by Haman, who wanted to destroy the Jews. The king's complicity in the matter is conveniently and wisely omitted. Then she finishes off her plea with two rhetorical questions designed to tug on the king's heartstrings. With a heartfelt and emotional plea, Esther bemoans her complete inability to bear even the thought that such a calamity might come to her people. In fact, this is one of only two times in the book when Esther shows her emotions (the other being at 4:4), and both are when she is concerned, not for her own well-being, but for the plight of her people.[6]

This time, however, the matter is not as simple for the king as accepting an invitation to a banquet. As persuasive as Esther's request might be, the problem is that Persian law is irrevocable.[7] No matter how much the king may want to revoke Haman's edict, his hands are tied. All he can do is give her free reign to do whatever she can to counteract Haman's law. As he gave complete liberty to Haman to craft an edict, so now the king gives complete liberty to Esther and Mordecai to craft their edict. He says,

> Behold, I have given Esther the house of Haman, and they have hanged him on the gallows, because he intended to lay hands on the Jews. But you may write as you please with regard to the Jews, in the name of the king, and seal it with the king's ring, for an edict written in the name of the king and sealed with the king's ring cannot be revoked. (8:7–8)

The spirit of the king's response is wonderfully captured by David Clines's paraphrase:

> Write what you like, says the king, as long as it doesn't overturn, revoke, or contradict anything previously written. Write what you like to Jewish advantage, says the king, as long as you realize that Haman's decree still stands. Write what you like, says the king, it will bear my seal; but remember that so does every other official document, including Haman's letter. Write what you like, says the king, for I give up; the conundrum of how to revoke an irrevocable decree, as you, Esther have asked, is beyond me; but feel free to write what you like—if you can think of a way to reverse the irreversible.[8]

That is enough for Esther and Mordecai, and they waste no time. They immediately summon the royal secretaries and have them draft a counter-edict. They cannot overturn Haman's edict, but they can at least try to level the playing field. The edict is written to allow the Jews, on that fateful day, to assemble and protect themselves. They may do that by destroying, killing, and annihilating any armed men that come to attack them—or the women and children of those attackers. The inclusion of women and children in the counter-edict has (understandably) offended many readers, prompting some to offer creative solutions to avoid the plain reading.[9] However, the inclusion of women and children, though troubling, is necessary to mimic the wording and counteract the terms of Haman's original edict. It is essential if the Jews are to be given the very same terms that Haman gave their enemies. The needed symmetry between the two edicts requires it.

The counter-edict also gives the Jews the right to plunder their enemies, just as Haman's edict gave the enemies of the Jews the right to plunder them. In fact, the wording of Mordecai's counter-edict parallels almost exactly the language of Haman's edict in Esther 3:13. The difference, of course, is that Haman's edict was aggressive, ordering the people to go on the attack against the Jews, while Mordecai's edict is self-defensive, in essence giving the Jews permission to defend themselves against their attackers. According to Mordecai's edict, the Jews cannot go around killing and plundering whomever they like. They are permitted to fight only against those armed forces that attack them. Thus, Mordecai's edict perfectly counteracts Haman's edict and seeks to neutralize its effect.

Just as with Haman's edict, copies are now made of Mordecai's edict and they are issued as a decree in all 127 provinces, to each province in its own script and to each people in its own language. That the king is fully supportive of the edict is indicated by the fact that the copies are carried to the provinces by couriers who are mounted on swift horses used in the king's service and are riding out hurriedly, urged on by the king's command.

Also, just as with Haman's edict, Mordecai's edict is also posted in Susa the citadel. Now both edicts are published throughout the empire, and it only remains to be seen eleven months later which group, the Jews or their enemies, will prevail.

For those who are familiar with the events of the day, however, the answer is already clear. The fortunes of the Jews are on the rise, and the fortunes of their enemies are on the decline, a fact on full display when Mordecai leaves the presence of the king to go into the city of Susa. With elaborate detail, Mordecai's royal regalia are described. He is wearing royal robes of blue and white. On his head is a great golden crown. Draped over him is a robe of fine linen and purple. With the emphasis on the colors of gold, purple, blue, and white and on fabrics of fine linen, the description is reminiscent of the luxuriant decor of the king's first banquet (1:6). Clearly, Mordecai has come into the fullness of the king's favor. How things have changed! After Haman's edict, Mordecai went out into the midst of the city wearing sackcloth and ashes (4:1); now, after the second edict, he goes out into the midst of the city wearing royal regalia.

Seeing him, the residents of Susa immediately erupt with shouts and rejoicing. What a contrast! When Haman's edict was issued, the residents of Susa were thrown into confusion, and the king and Haman sat down to feast (3:15), but when Mordecai's edict is issued, the citizens of Susa become exuberant, and the Jews throughout the empire sit down to feast, celebrating with gladness and joy. In fact, so clear is the way the two edicts will eventually play out, as the rise of Mordecai and the fall of Haman have already anticipated, that many of the people throughout the empire declare themselves to be Jews. What a fitting reversal it is that a story which began with Esther concealing her Jewish identity out of fear has now come to a place where people all over the empire are adopting a Jewish identity out of fear!

## THE JEWS DESTROY THEIR ENEMIES (9:1–19)

Eventually, the 13th of Adar arrives. But before disclosing the group that would emerge victorious in the clash of the two edicts, the narrator piles up clause upon clause upon clause: "Now in the twelfth month, which is the month of Adar, on the thirteenth day of the same, when the king's command and edict were about to be carried out, on the very day when the enemies of the Jews hoped to gain the mastery over them . . ." Five clauses are piled on top of each other, almost as if to give the sense of just how many things have been stacked against the Jews and how agonizing is the wait to find out who will prevail. But finally the outcome is revealed: ". . . the reverse occurred: the Jews gained mastery over those who hated them." In other words, the very reversal that played out personally between Mordecai and Haman now plays out more widely between the Jews and their enemies throughout the empire. The Jews gather in their cities throughout all the provinces of the empire to lay hands on anyone who seeks their harm. In fact, they are not alone. All the nobles of the provinces, the satraps, the governors, and the king's administrators are now helping the Jews, perhaps supplying them with weapons, because they too have been stricken with fear because of what happened with Mordecai.

At the end of the first day, the Jews have found overwhelming success. They have killed and destroyed their enemies. In fact, the narrator notes that they have done as they pleased to those who hated them, conveying the sense of an almost effortless victory. This too is an amusing reversal. The book of Esther opened with each palace official doing as he pleased; now the Jews are the ones who are doing as they please.[10]

In doing as they please, the Jews kill five hundred men in Susa the citadel, as well as the ten sons of Haman—Parshandatha, Dalphon, Aspatha, Poratha, Adalia, Aridatha, Parmashta, Arisai, Aridai, and Vaizatha. In a story in which much of the narrative is driven by the concealment of people's identity, the naming of each of Haman's sons is startling, like a tenfold hammering of judgment against their wicked and devious father.

The execution of Haman's sons was necessary for another reason as well. In the ancient world, the execution of sons was a regular practice to eliminate any possibility that they would seek to avenge their father's death. And so, with their death, Haman's downfall is complete: "Not only is he killed, but his honor, his position, his wealth, and now his sons—all his boasts from his days of glory (5:11)—are stripped away."[11]

When the king hears the report of the overwhelming victory from Esther, he exclaims, "In Susa the citadel the Jews have killed and destroyed 500 men and also the ten sons of Haman. What then have they done in the rest of the king's provinces!" (9:12). The answer is that in the rest of the provinces, the Jews killed 75,000 of those who hated them. The king continues, "Now what is your wish? It shall be granted you. And what further is your request? It shall be fulfilled" (v. 12). In yet another reversal, the king, who previously gave Haman a blank check to do as he pleased, now effectively gives Esther her own blank check to do as she pleases.

Why the king would solicit another request from Esther is not entirely clear, but the solicitation is certainly fortuitous because the job is not yet done. Esther responds, "If it please the king, let the Jews who are in Susa be allowed tomorrow also to do according to this day's edict. And let the ten sons of Haman be hanged on the gallows" (v. 13). Without any follow-up questions (so typical of the king!), Ahasuerus grants the request and commands that it be done. So a decree is issued in Susa to allow a second day, the 14th of Adar, for the carrying out of the edict. On the second day, the Jews kill an additional 300 men in Susa.

To some, the request for a second day reveals a certain bloodlust in Esther. On this reading, Esther has won the victory on the first day, but she is not yet satisfied; she wants more time for more killing. However, some crucial details in the account are worth noticing because they temper this assessment in some important ways. First, the narrator indicates that the Jews did only what was permitted in Mordecai's edict, and it permitted only actions to neutralize the attacks that Haman had prescribed. One can hardly fault the Jews for this. On analogy, it would be similar to Jews in the Warsaw Ghetto during World War II rising up to kill the SS troops in the area.[12]

Moreover, the history of the conflict reinforces their need to neutralize this threat for good. Saul, Mordecai's ancestor, had been commanded not to spare the sword and not to take any spoil in his dealings with the Amalekites (1 Sam. 15:3); however, he did the opposite. He spared the sword and took the spoil. Now, generations later, because of that decision, the Jews are in the very situation they are in. As a result, it is at least understandable that the Jews would feel the pressing need to neutralize any threat in their own generation.

Second—once again providing a contrast to the actions of Saul many generations earlier—the author emphasizes three times that the Jews did not lay their hands on the plunder, even though they were entitled to it (9:10, 15, 16). The point is that the Jews are not becoming opportunistic and getting carried away. On the contrary, there is a certain amount of restraint in what they are doing. They are doing only what they have to do in order to protect themselves from their attackers and ensure their future safety.

Third, in mirroring Haman's original edict, the edict for the Jews to kill their attackers provided for them "to destroy, to kill, and to annihilate any armed force of any people or province that might attack them, children and women included" (8:11). However, the narrator notes that when the 13th of Adar arrived, "the Jews killed and destroyed 500 men" (9:6). Nothing is mentioned about women or children. Nor is the third and most comprehensive word in the destroy-kill-annihilate triad used to describe their actions. The implication is that the Jews killed only those who would have killed them, that is, only men who attacked them and only to the extent that was required to defend themselves. No opportunity was seized to take "innocent" life, legal though it may have been to do so. The same seems to have been true throughout the empire. The number of deaths is reported to be "75,000 of those who hated them" (9:16). But who are those who hated them? According to the first part of the verse, they are those against whom the Jews had specific need to defend themselves. Again, the implication is that the 75,000 killed refers specifically to the men who rose up to attack the Jews, not to defenseless women or children.

Finally, Esther does not request a second day to carry out the edict throughout the empire. She wants the second day only in the capital of Susa, and she wants only an extension of the rules that were in force during the first day. In other words, she is not requesting an open season on the enemies of the Jews. Her request is very specific and very limited: one more day, and only in the capital city of Susa. Presumably, there were still pockets of resistance and hostiles looking forward to a second round with the Jews. Since Haman's ten sons were living in Susa during the ten months between his execution and the 13th of Adar, opposition to the Jews was probably mounting over that period of time. In sum, Esther requests what is necessary for the Jews to achieve a complete victory and to ensure that Haman's threat against them is fully and lastingly neutralized. A second day is necessary to make sure that the tables are turned, not partially, but completely.[13]

During this second day, Haman's ten sons, who were executed on the 13th of Adar, are also hanged on the gallows. Like an emphatic exclamation point, this is the crowning act of the great reversal. With this, the tables have been completely turned. In Esther 5, after Haman was invited to a second banquet with the king and queen, he went home and bragged to his wife and friends about his surpassing glory. In boasting to them, he bragged about his vast wealth, about how the king had honored him above everyone else, and about his many sons. Now, every one of those boasts has been undone. His vast wealth has been given to Esther, his high position has been given to Mordecai, and his sons have been hanged on the gallows in public disgrace, just like their father.

## GOD'S PROVIDENTIAL REVERSAL

With that, the reversal is complete—dramatically, powerfully, and finally. The enemies of the Jews, spearheaded by Haman, had plotted to destroy them, but in the end the tables were turned and the Jews prevailed over their enemies. For centuries, the story of that reversal—of God's people being on the brink of annihilation, but being snatched from the jaws of death and given victory in the end—has provided a narrative of hope and reassurance. No matter how bleak a situation has looked or how daunting one's circumstances have been, there has been the precedent of Esther on which to lean. God's providential work to overturn Haman's devilish plot has been there to keep one's hopes alive—a reminder of God's ability to reverse the irreversible, even in the midst of the greatest of threats.

It is no wonder that many Jews in Europe during World War II cherished the book of Esther. Particularly those living under the tyrannical reign of the Nazis clung tightly to the message of hope in Esther. In the face of Hitler's "final solution," so eerily similar to Haman's plot centuries earlier, they could read and reread the story of Jews surviving despite a brutal despot's attempt to annihilate them. They could read the story of Esther and Mordecai and hold out hope that in the end God would turn the tables and that they would prevail and not their enemies. In fact, so powerful a narrative was it that Hitler banned the reading of the book of Esther, and the Nazis would kill on the spot any Jew in the prison camps caught in possession of it. Yet many Jews were able to produce copies from memory.[14]

For so many, however, the tables never did turn. For them, the story of Esther seemed to prove hollow. The chambers filled with gas, the bullets left gun barrels, and the gallows were built, but it was not Hitler, that modern-day Haman, who hung on them, but Jewish men, women, and children. Where was God with his providential reversal then?

The same could be asked after many pogroms in history. In the infamous St. Bartholomew's Day massacre in 1572 and its aftermath, thousands (estimates range from 5,000 to 30,000) of French Calvinists were slaughtered. Like Haman's desire to eliminate Mordecai, the precipitating cause was a desire by Charles IX to eliminate rival Protestant leaders, which he did through the actions of his Swiss guard. Not surprisingly, though without direct sanction from the king, many civilians followed his lead and began to hunt down Protestants themselves. When the king took responsibility for the leaders' deaths publicly in Parliament, the cause spread throughout the provinces, with many locals believing they were effectively being ordered by the king to hunt down Protestants in their own cities. (Though Charles had sent out orders to try to prevent more violence, his words undoubtedly fanned the flame of local tensions.)[15] As Protestants were slaughtered in the French provinces, many no doubt asked, where was God with a providential reversal? Why were they not spared in their provinces in the same way that the Jews in Persia were spared in theirs?

The same question could have been asked when many Christians were slaughtered by Roman emperors, such as Diocletian and Galerius, or when scores of Christians in the fourth century were massacred by the Persian king Shapur II, or when one and a half million Christians were murdered during the last century by Sudanese Muslims.

For all of them, where was God's providential reversal when the Hamans of their day were executing their brutal decrees? Where was their last-minute deliverance?

Perhaps we have found ourselves asking a similar question. In Jewish tradition, "Amalek is the epitome of evil on earth . . . [and] is the last roadblock before the triumph of God."[16] Early Christian interpreters, such as Augustine and Origen, also saw the Amalekites, one of whom was Haman, as representative of sin and evil more generally.[17] In that sense, all of us have experienced our own Hamans whenever we have been attacked by evil or its effects. Who has not faced the ruthless enemy of cancer or other disease, and prayed for God to reverse the threat? Who has not lost a loved one to senseless violence, the careless actions of a drunk driver, or a cruel attack from someone bent on their destruction, and wondered why the Haman in their world was able to carry out his diabolical plan? Who has not been assailed with one kind of evil or another, external or internal, and pleaded with God to deliver them, much as he delivered the Jews from Haman long ago? And then, when the deliverance does not come in time, who has not plaintively asked God, "Where was my last-minute deliverance?"

In the raw anguish of Auschwitz and all the other massacres, attacks, and tragedies, might one dare to say—as many have—that it was not just those who held on to the book of Esther in the Nazi prison camps who died, but the God hidden in the pages of Esther as well? Elie Wiesel, in his book *Night*, recalled:

> One day when we came back from work, we saw three gallows rearing up in the assembly place. . . . Three victims in chains—and one of them, the little servant, the sad-eyed angel. The SS seemed more preoccupied, more disturbed than usual. To hang a young boy in front of thousands of spectators was no light matter. The head of the camp read

> the verdict. All eyes were on the child. He was lividly pale, almost calm, biting his lips. The gallows threw its shadows over him. . . . The three victims mounted together onto the chairs. The three necks were placed at the same moment within the nooses. "Long live liberty!" cried the two adults. But the child was silent. "Where is God? Where is He?" someone behind me asked. At a sign from the head of the camp, the three chairs tipped over. Total silence throughout the camp. On the horizon, the sun was setting. . . . We were weeping. . . . Then the march past began. The two adults were no longer alive. Their tongues hung swollen, blue-tinged. But the third rope was still moving; being so light, the child was still alive. . . . For more than half an hour he stayed there, struggling between life and death, dying in slow agony under our eyes. And we had to look him full in the face. He was still alive when I passed in front of him. His tongue was still red, his eyes were not yet glazed. Behind me, I heard the same man asking: "Where is God now?" And I heard a voice within me answer him: "Where is He? Here He is—He is hanging here on this gallows."[18]

Might we dare to think the same thoughts under the shadow of Hiroshima and Nagasaki, with their catastrophic losses of innocent life?[19] Might we dare think the same thoughts under the shadow of Balkan genocide and Sudanese persecution and 9/11-styled terrorism, with their huge death tolls at the hands of modern day Hamans? Might we dare to think the same thoughts under the shadow of Chernobyl, with its destruction of life and land, forever scourged by the tragic combination of humanity's technological competence and incompetence? Where is the hope that God will turn the tables? Where is the narrative promise of the book of Esther in the shadowy places? Why did the tables not turn at Auschwitz or Hiroshima or Kosovo or Chernobyl? Why did they not turn in first-century Rome, fourth-century Persia, sixteenth-century France, or twentieth-century Sudan? Where was God then? Did he not, as Wiesel suggests, hang on the gallows? Did he not evaporate under the bombs? Did he not perish in the explosions? Did he not fall by the sword? Did he not expire in the cancer ward or die at the cruel hands of senseless violence and brutal attacks?

Perhaps those questions are not so very different from the ones being asked by the disciples of Jesus in the immediate aftermath of his crucifixion. Perhaps they too wondered why their own contemporary Hamans had been successful in their plot to kill, destroy, and annihilate their leader and Messiah. Perhaps they too asked where God was in the midst of all those tragic events and why he had not reversed the fates of Jesus and his enemies in the way he had done with Esther and Mordecai so many years before. Perhaps, like Wiesel, as he watched a young child hang on the gallows and decided that the only sensible conclusion was that God himself was dying before his eyes, the disciples of Jesus could only watch him hang on the cross and conclude with an irony as deep as the divine that, yes, God was dying before their eyes.

Indeed he was—not in the sense that Wiesel meant it, but in a much more profound and seemingly unthinkable sense. For, in the aftermath of that Good Friday, when the rocks split and darkness covered the earth and the sun stopped shining, creation stood with its mouth agape, left groping in the noontime night for signs of life and hope amidst the boundaries of blasphemy. For God himself, in Jesus of Nazareth, was crucified, dead, and buried. When, on the next day, that empty Saturday morning, the sun rose and nature ran its course, the unthinkable had happened. In Jesus, God lay dead in a grave. God had taken a body and now he lay cold in a tomb. And under the shadow of the cross, we can hear the anguished voices crying out, "Why did the tables not turn? Where is God now?" The only words left were the sad and resigned confession, "Here he is—he is lying here . . . in this stone sepulcher."

Yet even in that place—the very place of death, hopelessness, and irrevocable tragedy—God was able to open up a new future. On the third day, the stone was rolled away, new life was raised up from the sepulchers of death, and hope blossomed in the scorched and ashen earth of tragedy. For the tables do turn—maybe not before the gas is turned on or the bomb is detonated, maybe not before the sword is swung or the atom is split, maybe not before the life support is turned off or the cross is lifted, but deeper, much deeper still, in the fabric of death that is woven irrevocably into the tapestry of our lives and our cultures and our world—deep down, in the chambers, in the pits, in the ashes, yes, in the tomb itself. There the tables do turn, for the one who went down into the grave came up in glory. The one who was laid to rest emerged in resurrection power. The one who submitted himself to the emptiness of the tomb rose again and made the tomb empty.

It is the resurrection of Jesus, and only the resurrection, that anchors the truth of Esther. God does turn the tables. While sometimes it is before the 13th of Adar, it so often is after Good Friday. But the promise still stands secure. And that means that for all the tragedy in our world, in our culture, and in our lives, nothing is beyond the touch of the God of the resurrection. Deep down, in those places of death and hopelessness and despair, deep down there—*there*—God is at work, plunging his providential hands into the ashes of our mortality and into the soil of our despairing world and crafting the newness of resurrection, so that one day we will be able to stand together in a new world with new bodies and, having experienced his deliverance and redemption, will say to one another, "On this day, the enemies of death and evil and tragedy had hoped to overpower us, but now the tables are turned and we have the upper hand. For our God has given us life in the place of death, goodness in the place of evil, and beauty in the place of tragedy."

## FOR FURTHER REFLECTION

1. What things make you question whether God is really at work in the world?
2. What kinds of theological questions would the cross have prompted the disciples to ask? How are those questions similar to your own questions?
3. How does the resurrection of Jesus give us both comfort in the midst of our questions and a powerful lens through which to understand death, evil, and tragedy?

CHAPTER TEN

# AN ONGOING CELEBRATION (9:20–10:3)

*God does not work wonders for a day, but to be had in everlasting remembrance. (Matthew Henry[1])*

After the tables had been turned and the Jews had gained the victory over those who hated them, there was cause for great celebration, but the celebration in the capital of Susa took place a day after the celebrations in the rest of the empire. In the rest of the empire, the Jews gained a complete victory by the end of the first day, the 13th of Adar. However, in Susa, where the pockets of hostilities were stronger, it took two days to gain the victory, the 13th and 14th of Adar.

## THE ESTABLISHMENT OF PURIM (9:20–32)

When it was all over, the Jews in the empire rested and celebrated with feasts on different days. In all the provinces of the empire, the 14th of Adar was the day of rest and celebration after the victory. But in Susa, it wasn't until the 15th of Adar that the Jews could rest and celebrate. Quite significantly, with these two celebrations, the book of Esther comes full circle. The book began with the celebration of two feasts, the first for the whole empire and the second for just the residents of Susa. Now, in perfect parallel with the beginning of the book, the story ends with two days of feasting, the first for the Jews throughout the whole empire and the second for the Jews just in Susa.

In light of these events, Mordecai thinks that this miraculous deliverance should be celebrated not just once, but as an annual festival. The logistical question, however, is when to celebrate it. Should it be celebrated on the 14th of Adar, when those around the empire first celebrated, or should it be celebrated on the 15th of Adar, when those in Susa first celebrated? Should one take priority over the other? Mordecai doesn't think so. So he sends out a record of the events and a letter to all the provinces, recognizing both dates as legitimate. By obliging them to keep both the 14th and the 15th of Adar, Mordecai may be proposing that everyone keep both dates (making it a two-day festival) or he may be proposing that those around the empire can celebrate the one-day festival on the 14th of Adar and those in Susa can celebrate the one-day festival on the 15th of Adar. Either way, the point seems to be that both dates are legitimate for the celebration. In fact, even today both days continue to be celebrated. Around the world, Jews continue to celebrate Purim on the 14th of Adar, except those living in one of the traditionally walled cities in Israel, such as Jerusalem; they celebrate Purim on the 15th of Adar, in keeping with the original practice.[2] In a similar way, Mordecai wants the people to recognize that both days have legitimacy. Now that is not just some shrewd political move to appease everyone. It's something much more significant, something theological. The point is that God's people should celebrate *in a spirit of unity.* After all, their deliverance was the same, and they are one people with one God. There is solidarity among them. Therefore, when they celebrate their deliverance, they should do so with mutual respect and in a spirit of unity.

In observing Purim, the people are to do two things. First, they are to celebrate by feasting. How appropriate! The events leading to the establishment of this holiday were characterized by feasting from beginning to end. In fact, the feasts in the book of Esther form a kind of thematic skeleton for the whole story, in the form of a chiasm:[3]

A. The king's feast for the officials of the empire (1:2–4)
  B. The king's feast for the men of Susa (1:5–8)
    C. The feast celebrating Esther's rise (2:18)
      D. Esther's first feast for the king and Haman (5:4–8)
      D' Esther's second feast for the king and Haman (7:1–10)
    C' The feast celebrating Mordecai's rise (8:17)
  B' The feast of Purim for Susa (9:18)
A' The feast of Purim for the whole empire (9:17, 19)

Thus, nothing could be more fitting than for feasting to be the main event in Purim celebrations in the years to come.

Second, the people are to give gifts of food to one another, as well as to the poor. Again, this is fitting. The holiday was established through events that threatened to take everything from them, as their enemies plotted to put them to death and plunder all their goods. In remembering those events, the people were to send their goods away to those who were deprived of them. By caring for the poor, the people would be reminded of how they would have lost everything if not for God's providential goodness to them.

Though the practices of the festival derive from the broad themes of the story, the name of the yearly celebration, interestingly enough, derives from one specific element in the story. The festival is called Purim, which is the word for "lots," as in "the casting of lots." At first, that might seem like an odd name for the festival. For one thing, the casting of lots is mentioned only once in the entire book (3:7), and it plays a relatively minimal role in the story. In fact, if the incident were removed from the book, the overall story line would remain intact. Not only that, but the one time that the lot is mentioned is when Haman calls the diviners to determine the best day to carry out his planned extermination of the Jews—a rather curious detail from which to derive the name of the festival. Why would anyone name a festival after the instrument their enemy used to set the date for their slaughter? Why name this festival Purim?

The reason may have to do with the larger theological issue raised by the casting of lots. Since God is not mentioned at all in the book, it might have been very tempting for the Jews to look back on the events and say that it was all just good luck. They may have been tempted to think that the little turns of event were no more than just chance occurrences that ended up working out in their favor. However, by naming the festival "Purim," attention is focused on something deeper. And it is this: the lot, or destiny, of God's people is not left up to chance and it is not determined by someone like Haman casting lots before his gods. No, only God determines the lot of his people. The name reminds the people that it is God and God alone who determines how things turn out in our world. Neither random chance nor chaotic forces nor competing powers do that. It is God and God alone who determined the lot of his people in Persia back then, and it is God and God alone who continues to determine the lot of his people in every generation.

For that reason, Mordecai sends out letters to all the Jews in the Persian provinces, insisting that because of everything that has happened, they should firmly obligate themselves and their future generations to keep those two days every year as days of remembrance. In response, the Jews firmly obligate themselves to do just that, a most fitting resolution to the narrative tension driving the overall story. Throughout the book, the Jews have been threatened by an edict that could not be revoked, but now they celebrate their deliverance from that threat with another ordinance that cannot be revoked. And this time it is the Jews who irrevocably bind themselves!

Then Queen Esther gives her own written authority to the establishment of Purim by sending a second letter, along with Mordecai, to all the Jews throughout the provinces of Persia, obligating them to keep the festival. She ties the feasting and celebrating to the rituals of fasting and lamenting. This will become important because even though mourning on the days of celebration will be forbidden, "the traditional fasting and lamentations serve to remind Israel of the background of Purim and provide the proper context for the season of joy."[4] Thus, her letter not only confirms the first letter, but adds a new and significant element to the observance of Purim by setting it in a wider context.

Moreover, her letter not only confirms and advances the previous letter that Mordecai sent, but also more fully reinforces her own identity. The narrator notes at this point that she is the daughter of Abihail, only the second time he has noted her Jewish father. The first time, in 2:15, when Esther was being brought into the palace to compete for a place as the new queen, she was identified by both her Persian name and her Hebrew name, as if to note that she was a young woman torn between two identities. Now, however, she may be the Persian queen, but her identity is defined by her Jewish ancestry, just as Mordecai is identified as "Mordecai the Jew."

Furthermore, her giving authority for a letter obligating the Jews to celebrate Purim also nicely rounds off the book with a humorous irony. At the beginning of the book of Esther, a letter goes out to the entire empire, insisting that wives be kept in their place (1:22); at the end of the book of Esther, a letter goes out to the entire empire, with the king's own wife issuing the final command![5]

## THE HIGH HONOR OF MORDECAI (10:1–3)

After the dual letters establishing Purim have been sent to all the provinces, King Ahasuerus imposes a tax on the land and on the coastlands of the sea. Literally, the king "sets" or "places" a tax on the land and the coastlands. In fact, the Hebrew word for "set" or place" (*sm*) is used only four times in the story, each of an action of the king and each marking a significant development in the unfolding of events. The first time the word is used is when the king "sets" the royal crown on Esther's head, making her the new queen (2:17). The second time is when the king "sets" Haman above all the other officials in his kingdom (3:1). The third time is when the king "sets" the crown on Mordecai's head after giving him the signet ring that he previously gave to Haman (8:2). Each of these times the king honors one of the three main characters in the plot. Now, at the very end of the book, the king "sets" something on everyone in the kingdom.

But why does he set taxes, a seemingly burdensome imposition, in contrast to the three previous settings? From a practical perspective, it is hard to be entirely sure, though it may have to do with compensating the crown for the costly losses incurred during the Haman-initiated conflict. Or it may simply be the reinstatement of the taxes that were suspended at Esther's coronation (2:18). But from a literary perspective, and more importantly, the imposition of the tax ties the end of the story back to the beginning. The story began with the king's insatiable appetites, in luxuriant surroundings and opulent feasting. The story ends with a (yet another) dig at the Persian king. Everything in the empire has changed: the fate of the Jews has been reversed, the enemies of the Jews have been conquered, and many non-Jews have declared themselves to be Jews (8:17). Throughout the empire, everything has changed; nothing has stayed the same—except, that is, the king! He is still the same self-indulgent man he was in the beginning.

The ground has completely shifted under his feet, and yet he remains exactly as he was—caring only to satisfy his own appetites.

Mordecai, however, is not the same. At long last, Mordecai's name and deeds are recorded in the king's annals (10:2), rectifying the previous oversight (6:1). All of his power and accomplishments are immortalized in Persia's records and, in the end, Mordecai the Jew is established as second in rank to King Ahasuerus in the entire Persian Empire, an honor previously enjoyed by his archenemy Haman. With this, not only is Haman's descent complete, but so is Mordecai's ascent. He is great among the Jews, and he is popular with his own people, for "he sought the welfare of his people and spoke peace to all his people" (10:3).

## CELEBRATING PURIM

So it was that Purim became a significant part of the Jewish year, established to bring the people together in celebration every year, reinforcing their solidarity with one another as they commemorated how the Lord had worked so providentially to thwart Haman, to establish justice, to redeem them, and to give them relief from their enemies.

Actually, it serves a very important purpose within the larger pattern of the Jewish year.[6] Purim, with its double feast, not only brings the book of Esther full circle, but also brings the whole Jewish year full circle. In the Jewish calendar, the year begins and ends around March. It begins with a celebration of the Passover and ends with a celebration of Purim. That is, it begins with a celebration of how God delivered his people from the oppression of Pharaoh in a foreign land, and it ends with a celebration of how God delivered his people from the oppression of Haman in a foreign land. Purim and Passover are bookends, marking the whole religious calendar of the people as a celebration of one long story of deliverance, as one grand sweep of God's redemptive work, from beginning to end.

Not only does Purim provide a bookend to the yearly liturgical calendar, but it provides another bookend as well. In the Old Testament, redemptive history originates with God's call to Abraham. Interestingly enough, God's call came while Abraham was in Ur, a city not too far from Susa. In calling Abraham, God also promised him that he would be a blessing to the whole world. So, in obedience, Abraham set out from Ur, walking across the whole known world, the Fertile Crescent, until he came to Egypt. The rest of the Old Testament is one long retracing of that journey, both historically and liturgically. God's deliverance of his people begins in Egypt—marked by the Passover—and it sweeps all the way back across to Persia, where a deliverance through Esther takes place—marked by Purim. And so, Purim brings everything full circle. It perfectly rounds off the liturgical year and the redemptive history it celebrates.

Over time, the festival of Purim gained in importance and pageantry.[7] The earliest mention of the feast of Purim outside the book of Esther dates from the second century B.C., but by the first century A.D. it is clear that the feast was widely celebrated around the region of Palestine and that the Esther scroll was being read during the festival. According to the Mishnah (the first major work of rabbinic Judaism, reflecting debates within Judaism from the first century B.C. to the second century A.D.), when the scroll of Esther was read for Purim, even the priests who were ministering in the temple were required to stop their sacrificial duties and listen to the reading. In fact, being present for the reading of the scroll was so important that the only acceptable reason for postponing the reading was to bury the dead. By the middle of the second century A.D., strict rules had developed to regulate the activities of the festival's celebration, and the reading of the scroll became the central feature on the morning of Purim.

During the third century, more symbolic aspects of the reading were introduced. One rabbi ordered scribes to begin writing the names of Haman's sons on ten separate lines, so that each name was directly under the preceding name. Just as a wall built with bricks stacked directly on top of one another would easily collapse, so the formatting of the scroll would give the sense of how easily the ten wicked sons collapsed. Another rabbi suggested that the names of the sons be written at the beginning of the line and that the word *the* be written at the end of the line, with a blank space between them, to symbolize the "large beginning" and the "small end" that each of them had.

Other innovations developed for the actual reading of the names. When the reader of the scroll reached the list of Haman's ten sons, the names were uttered very quickly, in one breath, to symbolize their joint execution. Then, when the reader reached the last name in the list, he was to lengthen the sound of the first letter to aurally give the sense of a long pole.

In the fourth century, one rabbi recommended that each person "drink until he knows not the difference between 'Cursed be Haman' and 'Blessed be Mordecai.' " More scrupulous authorities recommended that one not drink quite that much, but merely enough to fall asleep and not tell the difference.

As time went on, other practices accrued to the reading of the scroll in particular and to the celebration of the festival more generally. Whenever Mordecai's name was uttered, the congregation would whisper, "The memory of the righteous shall be a blessing," and whenever Haman's name was uttered, they would whisper, "The name of the wicked shall rot." Similarly, beginning in the fourteenth century, children began using rattles or stones during the reading to drown out the sound of Haman's name. In several European countries during the Middle Ages, children would draw the name or image of Haman on stones or wood and knock them together. Others would write his name on the soles of their shoes and stomp their feet whenever Haman's name was uttered during the reading of the scroll.

In some locations, even harsher treatments of Haman developed. At least as early as the fifth century, the burning of Haman in effigy and "beating" him became a popular pastime, apparently originating in Babylonia or Persia. This took various forms in various places. In one German town in the eighteenth century, a house of wax, with costumed wax figures of Haman, his wife, and two guards were placed on the reader's desk in the synagogue. When the reading began, the figures were set on fire. One nineteenth-century Russian describes a practice that developed in a town of the Caucasus:

> On Purim, when the men return home from reading the Scroll of Esther in the synagogue, the women prepare a black piece of wood in the kitchen by the fire. When the man comes into the room he asks his wife what it is, and she says, "It is Haman." At once the man gets angry and begins to scream at his wife that she should burn it. After kicking it, they all throw it into the fire.[8]

Even today, in places like Iran, Kurdistan, and Tel Aviv, an effigy is still doused with flammable liquid and set on fire while people stand around clapping and singing.

Beginning in the twelfth century in Italy and southern France, Purim was celebrated with the performance of plays, parodies, and frivolous monologues in private homes and public places. These performances typically flaunted or satirized Jewish practice and teaching, as well as inverted commonly accepted social norms. Teachers were mocked, social and religious authorities were derided, and popular Jewish culture was parodied. By the sixteenth century at the latest, people would masquerade in colorful costumes, with participants often dressing up like one of the characters in the story. Normal propriety was relaxed and ordinary rules of gender identity were temporarily set aside. Some men and women would wear clothes of the opposite sex, masks would be donned to conceal one's face, and childish tricks would be played on each other. Children would paint their faces and go from house to house, singing and dancing.

Throughout the centuries, the carnivalesque celebrations, with their sense of joy, playfulness, and levity, have provided a kind of festal antidote to the somber and terrifying circumstances of the original threat and the distressing circumstances of later threats in history. Perhaps that is why the festival has had such an enduring and powerful life in Judaism. In fact, as has been pointed out,

> the frequent bitterness of life in unfriendly diaspora lands made Purim increasingly meaningful to the Jewish people. Very early, they broadened its application and give it universal meaning by connecting it with God's vow . . . to destroy Amalek, the prototype of cowardice and evil. It is therefore easy to understand why a rabbi, many centuries ago, declared that even after the arrival of the Messiah, Purim would survive as a holiday to be observed by all mankind.[9]

## PROVIDENCE, DELIVERANCE, AND CELEBRATION

Perhaps Christians should reconsider the significance of Purim in light of the Messiah's coming. The meaning of Purim, biblically and historically, can be summarized in two ways. First, Purim celebrates God's hidden providence in bringing everything to its rightful conclusion. Esther is a story of everything looking hopeless, but being reversed by God's gracious but subtle providence. Evil may look like it is winning, but God will have the final victory. Hamans may lay their wicked plans, but, in the end, God will turn those plans back on their heads.

Second, Purim enables people to cope with the experience of exile. In fact, Purim

> is the only time, the only festival, that Judaism has structured for dealing with exile. While the three pilgrimage festivals deal with history, they do not deal with exile. Neither do the high holidays. The liturgies of those high holidays have reference to exile but their concern is not exile. . . . Since Judaism's arena is the arena of history, and exile is an aspect of Jewish existence, Judaism must deal with it. Exile must be grasped existentially. Purim does that. It is the enacting of exile.[10]

The second meaning obviously relates to the first. Exile is the experience of disorder, displacement, and chaos. It is a time when nothing makes sense, when home is far away, when the world is not as it should be. Yet the message of Purim is that God is still in control. God is working behind the scenes, carrying out his providential plans. Knowing that enables us to remember that though things may look grim, we can still smile with the confidence that God is in control. We can even celebrate in the darkness, for there is the promise that God is bringing the light. Even when the world is chaotic and seems to be falling apart, there is the assurance that God is holding it together and bringing it to its rightful conclusion. In short, Purim is about meeting the pain of our exile with the celebration of God's providence.

Perhaps, then, it is a bit surprising that the New Testament writers never quote from the book of Esther. However, there may be at least one allusion to it, and there are certainly more than a few thematic connections. In 2 Thessalonians 1, Paul may allude to the story of Esther, or at least to the themes of Esther.[11] Given the situation in Thessalonica, it is not hard to understand why. The Christians were facing serious threats and enduring harsh attacks. Like the Jews in Persia, their persecutors were threatening to end their lives and seize their property. Earlier, Paul had encouraged them to identify with Jesus in the midst of their sufferings, for he had been attacked in the same ways (1 Thess. 2:14–16). Nevertheless, Paul assures them that there will come a day of final justice (2 Thess. 1:5–12). Even now, he writes, the day of the Lord is drawing near, and on that day the situation will be reversed. Much like Haman and his followers, the enemies of the Christians in Thessalonica will "hang on their gallows"—or, as Paul puts it, "God will repay with affliction those who afflict you." Like the Jews in Persia, the Christians will be granted relief from those who are afflicting them and will enjoy rest from their enemies, while their enemies receive the affliction that they deserve.

At the end of the New Testament, John adds an additional picture of what will happen when that day comes. After evil has been conquered, persecutors have been punished, and justice has been served (Rev. 18), the people of God will sit down for—what else?—a banquet. But this will be a banquet like no other, not even the most joyous and exuberant Purim celebration. There will be feasting like never before, not even at the most extravagant Persian table. Words and deeds will be recorded that will tower above all others, even those recorded in the Book of the Chronicles of the Kings of Media and Persia. Quite simply, it will be the celebration to end all celebrations, a feast to end all feasts, a banquet to end all banquets, for at this banquet the deliverance will be eternal and the relief will be forever. As John describes it,

> After this I heard what seemed to be the loud voice of a great multitude in heaven, crying out,
>
> "Hallelujah!
> Salvation and glory and power belong to our God,
> for his judgments are true and just;

for he has judged the great prostitute
who corrupted the earth with her immorality,
and has avenged on her the blood of his servants."

Once more they cried out,

"Hallelujah!
The smoke from her goes up forever and ever."

And the twenty-four elders and the four living creatures fell down and worshiped God who was seated on the throne, saying, "Amen. Hallelujah!" And from the throne came a voice saying,

"Praise our God,
all you his servants,
you who fear him,
small and great."

Then I heard what seemed to be the voice of a great multitude, like the roar of many waters and like the sound of mighty peals of thunder, crying out,

"Hallelujah!
For the Lord our God
the Almighty reigns.
Let us rejoice and exult
and give him the glory,
for the marriage of the Lamb has come,
and his Bride has made herself ready;
it was granted her to clothe herself
with fine linen, bright and pure"—

for the fine linen is the righteous deeds of the saints.

And the angel said to me, "Write this: Blessed are those who are invited to the marriage supper of the Lamb." And he said to me, "These are the true

> words of God." Then I fell down at his feet to worship him, but he said to me, "You must not do that! I am a fellow servant with you and your brothers who hold to the testimony of Jesus. Worship God." For the testimony of Jesus is the spirit of prophecy. (Rev. 19:1–10)

In the meantime, as we wait and long for that day, we continue to live as exiles in this world (1 Peter 1:1, 17; 2:11). We too live in a world that is not our own home. We too live as sojourners on this earth. We too live in chaotic times, in which things are not as they should be. Hardship, pain, and a sense of displacement are more often the rule than the exception. Everyone struggles with living in a broken world and has times when they simply long to go home. Everyone knows the feeling that exile is the essence of their existence.

And so Purim continues to be of relevance to us. As we live in exile in this world, as we hope in the feast to come, as we rest in the undergirding strength of knowing that God is providentially working behind the scenes, we too can celebrate in anticipation. We can "rejoice in our sufferings, knowing that suffering produces endurance, and endurance produces character, and character produces hope, and hope does not put us to shame" (Rom. 5:3–5). Trusting in his providence at work, we can "know that for those who love God all things work together for good, for those who are called according to his purpose" (Rom. 8:28). When faced with the question, "Who shall separate us from the love of Christ? Shall tribulation, or distress, or persecution, or famine, or nakedness, or danger, or sword?" (Rom. 8:35), we can still celebrate the glorious truth that "neither death nor life, nor angels nor rulers, nor things present nor things to come, nor powers, nor height nor depth, nor anything else in all creation, will be able to separate us from the love of God in Christ Jesus our Lord" (Rom. 8:38–39).

Celebrating Purim today means rejoicing that Christ has come and that evil has been dealt its decisive deathblow. It means living with joy that the victory is already accomplished and will soon become a concrete reality in this world. It means that while we do not minimize evil or trivialize suffering, we nevertheless have a sense of lightheartedness and even playfulness in this life. So often, Christians can be stuffy, stoic, and stolid. Far too often our lives show scarcely any evidence of celebratory delight. Far too often we are uptight and take ourselves much more seriously than we really should. But the spirit of Purim reminds us that we shouldn't take ourselves all that seriously. Or perhaps a better way to put it is that Purim reminds us that we should take Christ and the good news of salvation so seriously that we don't take ourselves too seriously. We should be so overwhelmed by the good news that Christ has come, that Christ reigns, and that Christ is coming again, that we are able to hold our own lives with a looser grip than we often do. We should be so encouraged by the good news that God's providential plans are unfolding every day in our lives and in our world that we can be a little more lighthearted about the ups and downs we face on a daily basis. We should be so affected by the good news that God's purposes are going forward that we become a little more easygoing ourselves. Concisely put, the spirit of Purim ought to be alive and well today in the hearts of Christians, with all its joy, playfulness, delight, and even fun.

But our hearts can be filled with the spirit of Purim only as we live in the reality and conviction that one day Jesus will return and bring us into the realm of his perfect peace and joy and rest, and on that day we will sit down at a celebratory feast like we have never seen before. It is what John describes as the marriage supper of the Lamb, with glory and beauty that surpass that of the great Persian marriage banquet at the beginning of Esther and that of the merry Purim festival at the end of Esther. And we will celebrate. We will celebrate because we will be able to look back over the history of our world and the journey of our lives, and we will see before our eyes, for the first time, the full beauty of God's providential work. We will be able to look closely and see our own individual stories fitted together and playing their part in one larger mosaic of God's providential and redemptive work, so that all of history itself emerges before our eyes as one grand work of art more beautiful than anything Rembrandt could have painted. Together we will look deeply into its shapes and contours, and we will see the subtlety of its artistic style and the character of its brushstrokes. We will even find them in some of the most unexpected places—in our moral failures and our compromises, in our sufferings and our victimizations, in our moments of crisis and our defining moments, and in every twist and every turn of every seemingly insignificant and mundane detail. On that day, after having taken it all in, we will be able to rejoice with joy indescribable. We will celebrate with hearts overflowing. On that glorious day, we will see the artwork for what it really is: the masterpiece of the Artist himself. And we will see that in all the details of our lives, in all the events and in all the circumstances, he was providentially there. He was always there.

## FOR FURTHER REFLECTION

1. Why has Purim been such an important festival within Judaism?
2. Unlike other festivals in the Old Testament (such as Passover and Pentecost), Purim was never "translated" into Christianity. Why do you think that is?
3. What are some specific ways in which we can apply the spirit and meaning of Purim to our lives today?

# NOTES

## CHAPTER ONE: READING ESTHER

1 Blaise Pascal, *Pensées*, trans. A. J. Krailsheimer (New York: Penguin, 1995), 74.

2 Jack Sasson, "Esther," in *The Literary Guide to the Bible*, ed. Robert Alter and Frank Kermode (Cambridge, MA: Belknap, 1987), 341.

3 J. G. McConville, *Ezra, Nehemiah, and Esther*, Daily Study Bible (Louisville: Westminster John Knox, 1985), 174.

4 Hershel Shanks, "Losing Faith: Who Did and Who Didn't," *BAR* 33, no. 2 (March–April 2007): 50–57. The scholar was Bart Ehrman.

5 Daniel Howard-Snyder and Paul K. Moser, "Introduction: The Hiddenness of God," in *Divine Hiddenness*, ed. Daniel Howard-Snyder and Paul K. Moser (New York: Cambridge University Press, 2002), 1, 3.

6 This threefold distinction is made by Amelia Devin Freedman, *God as an Absent Character in Biblical Hebrew Narrative: A Literary-Theoretical Study*, Studies in Biblical Literature 82 (New York: Peter Lang, 2005), 167.

7 See Francis C. Rossow, "Literary Artistry in the Book of Esther and Its Theological Significance," *Concordia Journal* 13, no. 3 (1987): 226; Gregory R. Goswell, "Keeping God Out of the Book of Esther," *Evangelical Quarterly* 82, no. 2 (April 2010): 102.

8 See Alice Bach, *Women, Seduction, and Betrayal in Biblical Narrative* (New York: Cambridge University Press, 1997), 189.

9 Timothy K. Beal, *The Book of Hiding: Gender, Ethnicity, Annihilation, and Esther* (London: Routledge, 1997), 117, 129.

10 Babylonian Talmud, *Megillah* 7a; quoted in Meir Sternberg, *The Poetics of Biblical Narrative: Ideological Literature and the Drama of Reading* (Bloomington: Indiana University Press, 1987), 58–59. The same point has been made more recently by Forrest S. Weiland, "Literary Clues to God's Providence in the Book of Esther," *Bibliotheca Sacra* 160, no. 637 (January 2003): 38.

11 Sandra Beth Berg, *The Book of Esther: Motifs, Themes, and Structure*, Society of Biblical Literature Dissertation Series 44 (Missoula, MT: Scholars Press, 1979), 126.

12 Ludwig A. Rosenthal, "Die Josephsgeschichte mit den Buchern Ester und Daniel verglichen," *Zeitschrift für die alttestamentliche Wissenschaft* 15, no. 1 (January 1895): 278–84, and Moshe Gan, "The Book of Esther in Light of the Story of Joseph in Egypt," *Tarbiz* 31 (1961–62): 144–49, cited in Berg, *The Book of Esther,* 124–25.

13 Barry G. Webb, *Five Festal Garments: Christian Reflections on the Song of Songs, Ruth, Lamentations, Ecclesiastes, and Esther,* New Studies in Biblical Theology 10 (Downers Grove, IL: IVP Academic, 2000), 124–25. As Webb succinctly puts it in an earlier article, "Esther . . . testifies in a striking way to the fact that the absence of the miraculous does not mean the absence of God" (idem., "Reading Esther as Holy Scripture," *Reformed Theological Review* 52, no. 1 [January–April 1993]: 34).

14 This is developed at length by Richard Elliot Friedman, *The Disappearance of God: A Divine Mystery* (Boston: Little, Brown and Company, 1995), 7–140; see esp. 7–29. Much of what follows is dependent on Friedman's insights, as well as the unfortunately difficult to find George P. Burdell, "Hiddenness and Revelation: Theology and Typology," *Atlanta Theological Review*, no. 4 (1999): 126–42.

15 Samuel Terrien, *The Elusive Presence: Toward a New Biblical Theology* (Eugene, OR: Wipf and Stock, 2000), 470.

16 Karl Barth puts it well: "God is invisible and inexpressible because He is not present as the physical and spiritual world created by Him is present, but is present in this world created by Him in His revelation, in Jesus Christ, in the proclamation of His name, in His witnesses and sacraments. He is, therefore, visible only to faith and can be attested only by faith" (Karl Barth, *Church Dogmatics II.1: The Doctrine of God,* ed. G. W. Bromiley and T. F. Torrance [Edinburgh: T. & T. Clark, 1957], 190).

17 David Crump, *Knocking on Heaven's Door: A New Testament Theology of Petitionary Prayer* (Grand Rapids: Baker Academic, 2006), 281. Famously, Luther talked about divine hiddenness in two senses: God hidden in revelation (that is, revelation conceals God to all except those who have faith, because God is revealed in apparent weakness) and God hidden behind revelation (there is a hidden God that lies behind the revealed God, and God's will in the first may in fact contradict God's will in the second). The second sense has been criticized extensively; it is the first that is especially helpful in this discussion. See Alister McGrath, *Luther's Theology of the Cross: Martin Luther's Theological Breakthrough* (Oxford: Blackwell, 1985), 219–24; B. A. Gerrish, " 'To the Unknown

God': Luther and Calvin on the Hiddenness of God," *The Journal of Religion* 53, no. 3 (July 1973): 263–92.

18 See Timothy C. G. Thornton, "The Crucifixion of Haman and the Scandal of the Cross," *Journal of Theological Studies*, n.s., 37, no. 2 (1986): 419–26; Catherine Brown Tkacz, "Esther as a Type of Christ and the Jewish Celebration of Purim," *Studia Patristica* 44 (2010): 183–87.

## CHAPTER TWO: WILL THE REAL KING PLEASE STAND UP?

1 John Chrysostom, "Treatise to Prove that No One Can Harm the Man Who Does Not Injure Himself" in *Nicene and Post-Nicene Fathers: First Series*, vol. 9, ed. Philip Schaff (New York: Cosimo, 2007), 276.

2 The issue of Esther's historicity has been much discussed. A succinct summary of the arguments for and against can be found in Michael V. Fox, *Character and Ideology in the Book of Esther*, 2nd ed. (Grand Rapids: Eerdmans, 2001), 131–39. The standard arguments against the book's historicity can be found in Lewis B. Paton, *A Critical and Exegetical Commentary on the Book of Esther*, The International Critical Commentary (New York: C. Scribner's Sons, 1908), 64–77. See also Michael Heltzer, "The Book of Esther: Where Does Fiction Start and History End?," *Bible Review* 8, no. 1 (February 1992): 25–30, 41. For arguments that Esther is fundamentally historical, though written with a certain amount of literary artistry, see Karen H. Jobes, *Esther*, The NIV Application Commentary (Grand Rapids: Zondervan, 1999), 30–37; Robert Gordis, *Megillat Esther: The Masoretic Hebrew Text, with Introduction, New Translation, and Commentary* (New York: Ktav, 1974), 5–9; idem., "Religion, Wisdom and History in the Book of Esther—A New Solution to an Ancient Crux," *Journal of Biblical Literature* 100, no. 3 (September 1981): 359–388; Forrest S. Weiland, "Historicity, Genre, and Narrative Design in the Book of Esther," *Bibliotheca Sacra* 159, no. 634 (April–June 2002): 151–65. An argument against discounting Esther's historicity based on comparative chronology can be found in William H. Shea, "Esther and History," *Concordia Journal* 13, no. 3 (July 1987): 234–48. Some corroborating archaeological evidence can be found in Edwin Yamauchi, "Mordecai, the Persepolis Tablets, and the Susa Excavations," *Vetus Testamentum* 42, no. 2 (April 1992): 272–75; idem., "Archaeological Backgrounds of the Exilic and Postexilic Era, Part 2: The Archaeological Background of Esther," *Bibliotheca Sacra* 137, no. 546 (April–June 1980): 99–117.

3 For an introduction to Persian history during the fifth century, see Pierre Briant, *From Cyrus to Alexander: A History of the Persian Empire*, trans. Peter T. Daniels (Winona Lake, IN: Eisenbrauns, 2002), esp. 515–68; Lindsay Allen, *The Persian Empire* (Chicago: University of Chicago Press, 2005). For Persian history as it relates to the Bible, see Edwin M. Yamauchi, *Persia and the Bible* (Grand Rapids: Baker, 1990).

4 A. Leo Oppenheim, "On Royal Gardens in Mesopotamia," *Journal of Near Eastern Studies* 24, no. 4 (October 1965): 328–33.

5 The Hebrew word for "drink" is *shth*; the Hebrew word for "banquet" or "feast" is *mshth*. That drinking was the primary activity at such banquets, see Carey Ellen Walsh, "Under the Influence: Trust and Risk in Biblical Family Drinking," *Journal for the Study of the Old Testament* 25, no. 90 (September 2000): 17–18.

6 See Shimon Bar-Efrat, *Narrative Art in the Bible*, 2nd ed., Journal for the Study of the Old Testament Supplement Series 70 (Sheffield: Sheffield Academic Press, 1984), 195.

7 Timothy S. Laniak, "Esther," in Leslie C. Allen and Timothy S. Laniak, *Ezra, Nehemiah, Esther*, New International Biblical Commentary (Peabody, MA: Hendrickson, 2003), 193.

8 Elias Bickerman, *Four Strange Books of the Bible* (New York: Schocken, 1985), 186.

9 Jeffrey M. Cohen, "Vashti—An Unsung Heroine," *Jewish Bible Quarterly* 24, no. 2 (April–June 1996): 105.

10 The supposed irrevocability of Persian law plays a significant role in the book. However, it poses special problems, since no extrabiblical support can be found for it. Moreover, there seem to be logical and practical problems with the idea of irrevocable laws since, as Michael V. Fox writes, "it seems an impossible rule for running an empire" (*Character and Ideology in the Book of Esther*, 22). Ben Zion Katz argues, however, that the term does not designate irrevocability, but means that when the decree has gone out, there is no easy mechanism for recalling it or for reversing the effects of it. Understanding the term this way makes sense of the narrative, while also removing the historical and logical difficulties. See Ben Zion Katz, "Irrevocability of Persian Law in the Scroll of Esther," *Jewish Bible Quarterly* 31, no. 2 (April–June 2003): 94–96.

11 Samuel Wells, "Esther," in Samuel Wells and George Sumner, *Esther and Daniel*, Brazos Theological Commentary on the Bible (Grand Rapids: Brazos Press, 2013), 26–28.

12 This conflict between the worldly power of the Persian Empire and the transcendent, though invisible, power of God's kingdom

will play out in the rest of the book and is what drives much of the narrative tension. See Iain Duguid, "But Did They Live Happily Ever After? The Eschatology of the Book of Esther," *Westminster Theological Journal* 68 (2006): 85–98.

13 This is helpfully summarized in N. T. Wright, *Paul: A Fresh Perspective* (Minneapolis: Fortress, 2009), 62–65. The following readings of Philippians 3 and Romans 1 are likewise based on his insights.

14 The phrase is taken from Edward Welch's wonderfully titled book, *Addictions: A Banquet in the Grave, Finding Hope in the Power of the Gospel* (Phillipsburg, NJ: P&R Publishing, 2001).

15 This analogy is adapted from Peter van Inwagen, "What Is the Problem of the Hiddenness of God?" in *Divine Hiddenness*, ed. Daniel Howard-Snyder and Paul K. Moser (New York: Cambridge University Press, 2002), 24–32.

## CHAPTER THREE: A CINDERELLA STORY (ONLY SEEDIER)

1 John Calvin, "Isaiah 13:3," *Commentary on the Book of the Prophet Isaiah*, vol. 1, trans. William Pringle (Grand Rapids: Christian Classics Ethereal Library), available online at http://www.ccel.org/ccel/calvin/calcom13.xx.i.html.

2 Some have argued that the term "Jew" in the book of Esther should be understood as merely an ethnic designation and not a religious one, thus alleviating some of the discomfort of having a Jewish heroine who acts in ways inconsistent with Jewish morality. However, Anne-Mareike Wetter makes a strong case that the term should be understood to some extent as both ethnic and religious. See Anne-Mareike Wetter, "How Jewish Is Esther? Or: How Is Esther Jewish? Tracing Ethnic and Religious Identity in a Diaspora Narrative," *Zeitschrift für die alttestamentliche Wissenschaft* 123, no. 4 (December 2011): 596–603.

3 Esther 2:5–6 presents both historical and chronological problems because it would mean that Mordecai was at least 110 years old when Ahasuerus came to the throne, after which he served as a gatekeeper and an administrator. The usual suggestion is that this is a selective genealogy (as many biblical genealogies are), included mainly to establish Mordecai's Benjaminite ancestry, which will prove crucial in his conflict with Haman later in the story. For a discussion of the historical problems related to Mordecai, see Siegfried H. Horn, "Mordecai, A Historical Problem," *Biblical Research* 9 (1964): 14–25.

4 This view is argued in Jonathan Jacobs, "Characterizing Esther from the Outset: The Contribution of the Story in Esther 2:1–20," *Journal of Hebrew Scriptures* 8 (2008): 2–13.

5 See Leland Ryken, *Words of Delight: A Literary Introduction to the Bible*, 2nd ed. (Grand Rapids: Baker, 1993), 118–19; Edward L. Greenstein, "A Jewish Reading of Esther," in *Judaic Perspectives on Ancient Israel*, ed. Jacob Neusner, Baruch A. Levine, and Ernest S. Frerichs (Philadelphia: Fortress, 1987), 234; Timothy K. Beal, *The Book of Hiding: Gender, Ethnicity, Annihilation, and Esther* (London: Routledge, 1997), 35–36. André LaCocque points out that Daniel and his friends also have two names, which he sees as part of a larger concern for identity in the postexilic period. "The *Diasporanovelle* [a novella having to do with the Jews during their postexilic dispersion], be it the story of Joseph, or of Daniel, Judith, or Esther, describes a tense situation for the Jews in a foreign land. They must bear two names and two faces, have two calendars and two agendas, don two sets of clothing, eat at two tables, hold two discourses, live at the edge of two worlds" (André LaCocque, *The Feminine Unconventional: Four Subversive Figures in Israel's Tradition*, Overtures to Biblical Theology [Minneapolis: Fortress, 1990], 61).

6 See William F. Albright, "The Lachish Cosmetic Burner and Esther 2:12," in *A Light unto My Path: Old Testament Studies in Honor of Jacob M. Myers*, ed. H. N. Bream, R. D. Hein, and C. A. Moore (Philadelphia: Temple University Press, 1974), 25–32, esp. 31.

7 However, if Ahasuerus was away fighting battles during part of this time, which the chronology, when coordinated with historical records, may suggest, then the number would be smaller.

8 In the Septuagint version of Esther, the reference is Esther 14:15–17.

9 See Barry Dov Walfish, "Kosher Adultery? The Mordecai-Esther-Ahasuerus Triangle in Midrash and Exegesis," *Prooftexts* 22, no. 3 (Fall 2002): 305–33.

10 Iain M. Duguid, *Esther and Ruth*, Reformed Expository Commentary (Phillipsburg, NJ: P&R Publishing, 2005), 29.

11 Cited in Walfish, "Kosher Adultery?," 306.

12 Quoted in Oscar Cullman, *Salvation in History*, trans. S. G. Sowers (London: SCM, 1967), 125.

13 This story is told in Gordon MacDonald, "The Mark of the Artist" (sermon, October 16, 1994), text available online at http://www.csec.org/index.php/archives/23-member-archives/597-gordon-macdonald-program-3803. In telling the story, MacDonald assures his listeners that it is a true story, though he does not know the names of those involved.

## CHAPTER FOUR: HELL HATH NO FURY LIKE AN AGAGITE SCORNED

1 Thomas Watson, *A Body of Divinity* (Carlisle, PA: Banner of Truth, 1957), 112.

2 These are helpfully cataloged in Lewis B. Paton, *A Critical and Exegetical Commentary on the Book of Esther,* The International Critical Commentary (New York: C. Scribner's Sons, 1908), 186–88.

3 According to archaeological excavations conducted in the 1970s, "The gate was 40 by 28 meters (131 by 92 feet), covering about 1,200 square meters. Its central room was a square 21 meters (69 feet) at a side with four columns. There were two small rooms to the north and to the south, which were connected to the main hall by one-meter-wide doors. The height of the columns was probably about 12 to 13 meters (39 to 43 feet)" (Edwin M. Yamauchi, *Persia and the Bible* [Grand Rapids: Baker, 1996], 299).

4 Robert Gordis, "Studies in the Esther Narrative," *Journal of Biblical Literature* 95, no. 1 (March 1976): 47–48.

5 Frederic Bush, *Ruth/Esther,* Word Biblical Commentary 9 (Waco: Thomas Nelson, 1996), 374.

6 Verse 6 begins with the clause "who had been carried away from Jerusalem among the captives." Grammatically, it could refer either to Mordecai or to Kish. However, the most natural antecedent is Mordecai, since he is the one being identified. Kish, then, would not necessarily be the great-grandfather of Mordecai, but could be a more distant ancestor. Given that Haman is deliberately introduced as an Agagite, the identification of Kish with the father of Saul is almost assured. This kind of selective genealogy is not uncommon in the Bible.

7 This is persuasively argued in Ronald T. Hyman, "Esther 3:3: The Question with No Response," *Jewish Bible Quarterly* 22, no. 2 (April–June 1994): 103–9.

8 William W. Hallo, "The First Purim," *Biblical Archaeologist* 46, no. 1 (Winter 1983): 19–26.

9 This rhetorical strategy is pointed out by Carey A. Moore, *Esther: A New Translation with Introduction and Commentary,* The Anchor Bible 7 (Garden City, NY: Doubleday, 1971), 42. The explanation of the strategy is expanded in Michael V. Fox, *Character and Ideology in the Book of Esther,* 2nd ed. (Grand Rapids: Eerdmans, 2001), 47–51.

10 Joseph Fleishman, "Why Did Ahasuerus Consent to Annihilate the Jews?," *Journal of Northwest Semitic Languages* 25, no. 2 (1999): 56.

11 Marc Zvi Brettler, *How to Read the Bible* (Philadelphia: Jewish Publication Society, 2005), 268–69.

12 W. Lee Humphreys, "The Story of Esther and Mordecai: An Early Jewish Novella," in *Saga, Legend, Tale, Novella, Fable: Narrative Forms in Old Testament Literature*, ed. George W. Coats, Journal for the Study of the Old Testament Supplement Series 35 (Sheffield: JSOT Press, 1985), 105.
13 Bush, *Ruth/Esther*, 387.
14 Werner Dommershausen, *Ester* (Würzburg: Echter, 1980), 40.
15 N. L. Collins, "Did Esther Fast on the 15th Nisan? An Extended Comment on Esther 3:12," *Revue Biblique* 100 (1993): 547.
16 Karen H. Jobes, *Esther*, The NIV Application Commentary (Grand Rapids: Zondervan, 1999), 125.
17 John Foxe, *The New Foxe's Book of Martyrs* (North Brunswick, NJ: Bridge-Logos, 1997), 11–37.
18 Paul Marshall, Lela Gilbert, and Nina Shea, *Persecuted: The Global Assault on Christians* (Nashville: Thomas Nelson, 2013), 5.
19 Hassan Dehqani-Tafti, *The Hard Awakening* (New York: Seabury Press, 1981), 113–14. The early biographical details are given in Hassan Dehqani-Tafti, *Design of My World: Pilgrimage to Christianity* (New York: Seabury Press, 1982).

## CHAPTER FIVE: THE MOMENT OF TRUTH

1 Stephen Charnock, "A Discourse of Divine Providence," in *The Complete Works of Stephen Charnock*, vol. 1 (Edinburgh: James Nichol, 1864), 61.
2 Gary A. Anderson, *A Time to Mourn, a Time to Dance: The Expression of Grief and Joy in Israelite Religion* (University Park, PA: Pennsylvania State University Press, 1991), 87–91.
3 This point is made by Timothy Laniak. He compares this instance to the fasting in Jonah and argues that fasting before a disaster is "preventative fasting," which seeks to "move the hand of God to prevent it." Timothy S. Laniak, *Shame and Honor in the Book of Esther*, Society of Biblical Literature Dissertation Series 165 (Atlanta: Scholars Press, 1998), 91.
4 Elizabeth Groves, "Double Take: Another Look at the Second Gathering of Virgins of Esther 2.19a," in *The Book of Esther in Modern Research*, ed. Leonard Greenspoon and Sidnie White Crawford, Journal for the Study of the Old Testament Supplement Series 380 (London: T&T Clark, 2003), 92.
5 It is possible to render Mordecai's statement as an interrogative followed by a declarative: "For if you keep silent at this time, will relief and deliverance rise for the Jews from another place? Then you and your father's family will perish." This is not syntactically impossible, and it would make sense within the context. If this

is the right reading, then Mordecai is not expressing confidence that deliverance will come one way or another, but rather is pressing home the point to Esther that she is their only hope. See John M. Wiebe, "Esther 4:14: 'Will Relief and Deliverance Arise for the Jews from Another Place?,' " *Catholic Biblical Quarterly* 53, no. 3 (July 1991): 409–15.

6 David J. A. Clines, *The Esther Scroll: The Story of the Story*, Journal for the Study of the Old Testament Supplement Series 30 (Sheffield: JSOT Press, 1984), 36–37.

7 W. Lee Humphreys, "The Story of Esther and Mordecai: An Early Jewish Novella," in *Saga, Legend, Tale, Novella, Fable: Narrative Forms in Old Testament Literature*, ed. George W. Coats, Journal for the Study of the Old Testament Supplement Series 35 (Sheffield: JSOT Press, 1985), 106.

8 It is striking that the three days of Esther's fast, begun at Passover, were the same three days in the annual calendar as the days of Jesus' humiliation on the cross and in the grave. For Esther, the fast was a symbolic death. For Jesus, the cross was a literal death. See Michael G. Wechsler, "Shadow and Fulfillment in the Book of Esther," *Bibliotheca Sacra* 154, no. 615 (July–September 1997): 275–84.

9 Eric Metaxas, *Amazing Grace: William Wilberforce and the Heroic Campaign to End Slavery* (New York: HarperCollins, 2007), 113.

10 Michael V. Fox, "Three Esthers," in *The Book of Esther in Modern Research*, ed. Leonard Greenspoon and Sidnie White Crawford, Journal for the Study of the Old Testament Supplement Series 380 (London: T&T Clark, 2003), 52.

11 Eberhard Bethge, "One of the Silent Bystanders? Dietrich Bonhoeffer on November 9, 1938," in *Friendship and Resistance: Essays on Dietrich Bonhoeffer* (Grand Rapids: Eerdmans, 1995), 58–71, cited in Patrick D. Miller, "For Such a Time as This," *Princeton Seminary Bulletin*, n.s., 27, no. 2 (2006): 146–55. In what follows, I am leaving aside the important question of whether plotting the assassination of a mass murderer such as Hitler is or is not ethically justified. I only wish to highlight that Bonhoeffer sought to discern what role he might be called to play in the needs and crises of his day.

## CHAPTER SIX: STEP OF FAITH

1 Charles Haddon Spurgeon, "God's Providence" (sermon, New Park Street Chapel, Southwark, London, October 15, 1908), available online at http://www.spurgeon.org/sermons/3114.htm.

2 Karol Jackowski, "Holy Disobedience in Esther," *Theology Today* 45, no. 4 (January 1989): 407.

3 Bernard Rudofsky, *The Unfashionable Human Body* (Garden City, NY: Doubleday, 1971), 99.
4 See the treasury relief depicted in Edwin M. Yamauchi, *Persia and the Bible* (Grand Rapids: Baker, 1996), 360. A description is given on 360–62.
5 Leila L. Bronner, "Reclaiming Esther: From Sex Object to Sage," *Jewish Bible Quarterly* 26, no. 1 (January–March 1998): 7.
6 Yehuda Radday, "Esther with Humour," in *On Humour and the Comic in the Hebrew Bible*, ed. Yehuda T. Radday and Athalya Brenner, Journal for the Study of the Old Testament Supplement Series 92 (Sheffield: Almond Press, 1990), 305.
7 Linda M. Day, *Esther*, Abingdon Old Testament Commentary (Nashville: Abingdon, 2005), 94.
8 R. C. Sproul, *The Invisible Hand* (Dallas: Word, 1997), 210.

## CHAPTER SEVEN: THE PIVOT POINT

1 B. B. Warfield, *Biblical Doctrines* (Carlisle: Banner of Truth, 1988) 22.
2 Jon D. Levenson, *Esther*, Old Testament Library (Louisville: Westminster John Knox, 1997), 92.
3 Yehuda Radday, "Esther with Humour," in *On Humour and the Comic in the Hebrew Bible*, ed. Yehuda T. Radday and Athalya Brenner, Journal for the Study of the Old Testament Supplement Series 92 (Sheffield: Almond Press, 1990), 306.
4 Iain M. Duguid, *Esther and Ruth*, Reformed Expository Commentary (Phillipsburg, NJ: P&R Publishing, 2005), 75.
5 There is debate over whether the crown is to be set on Haman's head or on the horse's head. The syntax technically allows for either, but it would most naturally indicate the horse's head, and there are some ancient reliefs that may support this as a possible practice. However, it is not critical to the development of the story. For arguments on both sides of the issue, see any of the standard commentaries on Esther.
6 "A person's garment is considered a part of his body, or a part of his being. Tearing one's clothes in mourning is permitted, as a kind of substitute for injuring one's body (which is prohibited in Deut. 14:1–2); cutting off half of a person's garment and shaving off half his beard is a way of humiliating him without actually causing bodily harm (2 Sam. 10:4–5); when the army commanders spread their clothes on the stairs under Jehu they are signaling their submission and loyalty to him (2 Kings 9:13); Aaron's priestly garments are donned by Eleazar, his son, as he inherits the priestly office (Num. 20:25–28); Elijah's cloak symbolizes the prophetic office as well as the person of Elijah, and Elisha's receiving this

cloak means that he has replaced Elijah" (Adele Berlin, *Esther* [Philadelphia: Jewish Publication Society, 2001], 59).

7 Adele Berlin, "The Book of Esther and Ancient Storytelling," *Journal of Biblical Literature* 120, no. 1 (Spring 2001): 11.

8 David J. A. Clines, *Ezra, Nehemiah, Esther,* New Century Bible Commentary (Grand Rapids: Eerdmans, 1984), 307–8.

9 Berlin, *Esther,* 33.

10 Linda M. Day, *Esther,* Abingdon Old Testament Commentary (Nashville: Abingdon, 2005), 112.

11 The statistical distributions were suggested to me by Bruce Waltke. Karen Jobes also points out that the book refers three times to the annals of the king: once at the beginning (2:23), once at the end (10:2), and once at the center point of the story (6:1). Karen H. Jobes, *Esther,* The NIV Application Commentary (Grand Rapids: Zondervan, 1999), 157.

12 This structure is adapted with minimal changes from Jonathan Grossman, *Esther: The Outer Narrative and the Hidden Reading,* Siphrut 6 (Winona Lake, IN: Eisenbrauns, 2001), 14.

13 Frederick Buechner, *Now and Then: A Memoir of Vocation* (New York: HarperOne, 1983), 87.

14 J. C. Ryle, *Expository Thoughts on the Gospels: St. Luke* (New York: Robert Carter and Brothers, 1879), 2:61–62.

## CHAPTER EIGHT: POETIC JUSTICE

1 John Flavel, *Divine Conduct; or, The Mystery of Providence* (London: Religious Tract Society, 1847), 32.

2 Sandra Beth Berg, *The Book of Esther: Motifs, Themes, and Structure,* Society of Biblical Literature Dissertation Series 44 (Missoula, MT: Scholars Press, 1979), 101–2; Carol M. Bechtel, *Esther,* Interpretation (Louisville: John Knox, 2002), 42, 63–64. Of course, the wordplay works only in Hebrew, but in the narrative world of the story, it makes perfect sense.

3 Karen H. Jobes, *Esther,* The NIV Application Commentary (Grand Rapids: Zondervan, 1999), 165.

4 An alternative reading is that Ahasuerus knew perfectly well that Haman wasn't doing anything inappropriate but, needing an excuse to execute him for something other than the plot, in which he was also complicit, he seized on the opportunity presented by the appearances and accused Haman of rape. This is entirely possible, but by no means assured. After all, the king is characterized throughout the book of Esther as dim-witted and thoughtless. Given the established pattern of the king's behavior in the book so far, it seems more probable that he once again

jumps to an ill-founded conclusion without thinking through all the implications.

5 Edwin Yamauchi quotes one of the edicts on harem conduct published by Ernst Wiedner in 1954–1955 as stating: "A courtier or a eunuch when he would speak with a woman of the palace should not approach closer than seven steps. He may not speak with her if she is insufficiently clothed, nor may he remain standing and listening when two palace women are gossiping" (Edwin M. Yamauchi, *Persia and the Bible* [Grand Rapids: Baker, 1996], 262).

6 Linda M. Day, *Esther,* Abingdon Old Testament Commentary (Nashville: Abingdon, 2005), 113.

7 Adele Berlin, "The Book of Esther and Ancient Storytelling," *Journal of Biblical Literature* 120, no. 1 (Spring 2001): 14.

8 Stan Goldman, "Narrative and Ethical Ironies in Esther," *Journal for the Study of the Old Testament* 15, no. 47 (June 1990): 18.

9 William Shakespeare, *Hamlet,* in *The Complete Works of William Shakespeare,* vol. 2 (Garden City, NY: Nelson Doubleday, 1979), act 3, scene 4, lines 202–10.

10 John Owen, "The Death of Death in the Death of Christ," in *The Works of John Owen,* vol. 10 (Carlisle, PA: Banner of Truth, 1978), 157–421.

11 Augustine, "Sermon 263," in *Sermons: VII (230–272B),* trans. Edmund Hill, The Works of Saint Augustine, Part 3-7 (Hyde Park, NY: New City Press, 1993), 219–20.

12 Barry G. Webb, *Five Festal Garments: Christian Reflections on the Song of Songs, Ruth, Lamentations, Ecclesiastes, and Esther,* New Studies in Biblical Theology 10 (Downers Grove, IL: IVP Academic, 2000), 132.

13 Thomas Brooks, "A Heavenly Cordial," in *The Complete Works of Thomas Brooks,* vol. 6 (Edinburgh: James Nichol, 1867), 428.

14 N. T. Wright, *Evil and the Justice of God* (Downers Grove, IL: InterVarsity, 2006), 119.

## CHAPTER NINE: THE TABLES ARE TURNED

1 G. C. Berkouwer, *The Providence of God* (Grand Rapids: Eerdmans, 1952), 84–85.

2 Carol M. Bechtel, *Esther,* Interpretation (Louisville: John Knox, 2002), 70.

3 Adele Berlin, *Esther* (Philadelphia: Jewish Publication Society, 2001), 71.

4 Kristen De Troyer, *The End of the Alpha Text of Esther: Translation and Narrative Technique in MT 8:1–17, LXX 8:1–17, and AT 7:14–41,*

Society of Biblical Literature Septuagint and Cognate Studies Series 48 (Atlanta: Society of Biblical Literature, 2000), 92.

5 Werner Dommershausen, *Die Estherrolle: Stil und Zeil einer alttestamentlichen Schrift*, Stuttgarter Biblische Monographien 6 (Stuttgart: Verlag Katholisches Bibelwerk, 1968), 100.

6 Linda Day, *Three Faces of a Queen: Characterization in the Books of Esther*, Journal for the Study of the Old Testament Supplement Series 186 (Sheffield: Sheffield Academic Press, 1995), 177.

7 As was mentioned in chapter 2, footnote 10, irrevocability probably does not mean that a previous law could not be amended or even retracted; that would present a number of historical and logical difficulties. Instead, it most likely means that when a decree has gone out, there is no easy mechanism for recalling it or for reversing the effects of it. To use an analogy, it would be like spilling a bag of flour in the dirt. Theoretically, one could try to scoop up the flour and put it back in the bag, but one could never return the bag of flour to its original condition. Similarly, Persian law was likely understood to unleash ramifications and consequences in its passing, such that one could not return the matters of the empire back to the way things were beforehand. In this case, it would mean that trying to retract Haman's edict would only cause confusion within the empire, and there would still be those who would "obey" the original orders. See Ben Zion Katz, "Irrevocability of Persian Law in the Scroll of Esther," *Jewish Bible Quarterly* 31, no. 2 (April–June 2003): 94–96.

8 David J. A. Clines, *The Esther Scroll: The Story of the Story*, Journal for the Study of the Old Testament Supplement Series 30 (Sheffield: JSOT Press, 1984), 19.

9 For instance, Robert Gordis argues, "In reconsidering the passage, we may note that it is scarcely likely that the royal edict would permit the Jews to slaughter the women and the children of the general population. . . . The verse should, therefore, be rendered: 'By these letters the king permitted the Jews in every city to gather and defend themselves, to destroy, kill, and wipe out every armed force of a people or a province attacking them, their children and their wives, with their goods as booty' " (Robert Gordis, "Studies in the Esther Narrative," *Journal of Biblical Literature* 95, no. 1 [March 1976]: 50, 51–52). The NIV adopts the same reading as Gordis, but has been critiqued by numerous scholars for the implausibility of this reading. Joyce Baldwin argues for essentially the same reading, but on the grounds that the edict specifies those who would attack the Jews, which would hardly have included women and children. Joyce G. Baldwin, *Esther: An Introduction*

*and Commentary*, Tyndale Old Testament Commentary 12 (Downers Grove, IL: InterVarsity Press, 1984), 97–98. Again, the majority of scholars have not been persuaded. The reading that makes the most sense in terms of (1) the natural reading of the Hebrew, (2) the literary artistry of the story, and (3) the intertextual connections with 1 Samuel 15 (see especially vv. 2–3 and the comments below on Esther 9:1–19) is that the edict allows the Jews to strike down women and children as well as armed men. Whether they will avail themselves of that allowance is another matter, and we can at least be relieved that they do not.

10 Samuel Wells and George Sumner, *Esther and Daniel*, Brazos Theological Commentary on the Bible (Grand Rapids: Brazos Press, 2013), 85.

11 Michael V. Fox, *Character and Ideology in the Book of Esther*, 2nd ed. (Grand Rapids: Eerdmans, 2001), 110.

12 This analogy is suggested by André LaCocque, "Haman in the Book of Esther," *Hebrew Annual Review* 11 (1987): 219.

13 For a historical survey of whether the Jews' actions should be understood as revenge/vengeance or self-defense, and for an argument for the latter, see Haim M. I. Gevaryahu, "Esther Is a Story of Jewish Defense, Not a Story of Jewish Revenge," *Jewish Bible Quarterly* 21, no. 1 (January 1993): 3–12; Bruce William Jones, "Two Misconceptions about the Book of Esther," *Catholic Bible Quarterly* 39, no. 2 (April 1977): 171–81. Understanding the actions to be humorous hyperbole, Jones writes, "If an enemy did not attack the Jews first, he was in no danger. Who would be so foolish as to make himself subject to the second edict? It would be suicide to attack the Jews. Who would be so stupid as to observe Haman's obsolete edict, not knowing of the second one, published more efficiently? The answer is that 800 people in Susa and 75,000 in the provinces were so stupid!" (180). Another suggestion is put forward by Bardtke, who wonders whether the actions of the Jews might have further justification in the need to preserve the people who are the bearers of God's promise. This would entirely circumvent the potentially troubling question of whether the Jews' actions were normative and/or prescriptive. Instead, that would be historically contingent. Hans Bardtke, *Das Buch Esther*, Kommentar zum Alten Testament 17/5 (Gütersloh: Mohn, 1963), 384. For the view that the actions of Esther and the Jews should be read as morally reprehensible, but necessary at the literary level for the full ironic reversal of the narrative, see Stan Goldman, "Narrative and Ethical Ironies in Esther," *Journal for the Study of the Old Testament* 15, no. 47 (June 1990): 15–31.

Goldman points out that Esther was given two names earlier in the book, a Jewish name and a Persian name. We see in the carrying out of these actions an encapsulated reversal of identities. The Persians, out of fear, declare themselves to be Jews (8:17), while Esther, the Jew, acts like a Persian.

14 Karen H. Jobes, *Esther*, The NIV Application Commentary (Grand Rapids: Zondervan, 1999), 220; Philip Goodman, *The Purim Anthology* (Philadelphia: Jewish Publication Society, 1964), 374. Goodman also documents that in a speech given on January 30, 1944, Adolf Hitler declared that if the Nazis went down in defeat, the Jews could celebrate a triumphant second Purim. Tellingly, less than three years later (October 16, 1946), ten Nazi chieftains were hung on the gallows at Nuremberg, an act eerily similar to the hanging of Haman's ten sons. One of them clearly perceived the connection; when led to the scaffold, he shouted, "Purim Feast, 1946" (375–76).

15 Mack P. Holt, *The French Wars of Religion, 1562–1629* (Cambridge: Cambridge University Press, 1995), 85–92.

16 André LaCocque, *The Feminine Unconventional: Four Subversive Figures in Israel's Tradition*, Overtures to Biblical Theology (Minneapolis: Fortress, 1990), 70.

17 Augustine, "On the Holy Trinity," *Nicene and Post-Nicene Fathers: First Series*, vol. 3, ed. Philip Schaff (Peabody, MA: Hendrickson, 2004), 4.15.20; Origen, *Homilies on Numbers* (Downers Grove, IL: IVP Academic, 2009), 19.1.

18 Elie Wiesel, *Night*, trans. Stella Rodway (New York: Bantam Books, 1987), 61–62.

19 Much of what follows is influenced by Alan E. Lewis, *Between Cross and Resurrection: A Theology of Holy Saturday* (Grand Rapids: Eerdmans, 2001).

## CHAPTER TEN: AN ONGOING CELEBRATION

1 Matthew Henry, *Commentary on the Whole Bible, Volume II: Joshua to Esther* (Grand Rapids: Christian Classics Ethereal Library, 2009), 2003.

2 Philip Goodman, *The Purim Anthology* (Philadelphia: Jewish Publication Society, 1964), 143, 146, 440. Goodman cites the Mishnah, *Megillah* 1:1, as well as the book of Esther as precedent.

3 Adapted from Karen H. Jobes, *Esther*, The NIV Application Commentary (Grand Rapids: Zondervan, 1999), 155; Michael V. Fox, *Character and Ideology in the Book of Esther*, 2nd ed. (Grand Rapids: Eerdmans, 2001), 157; Sandra Beth Berg, *The Book of Esther: Motifs, Themes, and Structure*, Society of Biblical Literature Dissertation

Series 44 (Missoula, MT: Scholars Press, 1979), 31–57. Fox also notes two "minor" feasts as well, the feast that Vashti held for the women in 1:9 and the two-person feast that the king and Haman had in 3:15, after the decree was issued. Both, of course, contribute to the plot, but are not as indispensible to the narrative development as the other eight banquets.

4 Brevard S. Childs, *Introduction to the Old Testament as Scripture* (Philadelphia: Fortress, 1979), 604.

5 Linda M. Day, *Esther*, Abingdon Old Testament Commentary (Nashville: Abingdon, 2005), 162.

6 The following liturgical observations are based on Barry G. Webb, *Five Festal Garments: Christian Reflections on the Song of Songs, Ruth, Lamentations, Ecclesiastes, and Esther*, New Studies in Biblical Theology 10 (Downers Grove, IL: IVP Academic, 2000), 111, 127–28; Eugene Peterson, *Five Smooth Stones for Pastoral Work* (Grand Rapids: Eerdmans, 1980), 203–5.

7 The following historical and anecdotal information is drawn from Abraham P. Bloch, *The Biblical and Historical Background of the Jewish Holy Days* (New York: Ktav, 1978), 79–99; idem., *The Biblical and Historical Background of Jewish Customs and Ceremonies* (New York: Ktav, 1980), 279–92; Kenneth M. Craig Jr., *Reading Esther: A Case for the Literary Carnivalesque* (Louisville: Westminster John Knox, 1995), 156–68; Edward L. Greenstein, "A Jewish Reading of Esther," in *Judaic Perspectives on Ancient Israel*, ed. Jacob Neusner, Baruch A. Levine, and Ernest S. Frerichs (Philadelphia: Fortress, 1987), 231–232; Bradley C. Gregory, "Megillot and Festivals," in *Dictionary of the Old Testament: Wisdom, Poetry and Writings*, ed. Tremper Longman III and Peter Enns (Downers Grove, IL: IVP Academic, 2008), 457–64; idem, "Purim," in Longman and Enns, *Dictionary of the Old Testament*, 631–33; Philip Goodman, *The Purim Anthology* (Philadelphia: Jewish Publication Society, 1964), 7–8, 12–13, 321–329.

8 Goodman, *The Purim Anthology*, 323.

9 Solomon Grayzel as quoted in ibid., 12–13.

10 Monford Harris, "Purim, Celebration of Disorder," *Judaism* 26, no. 2 (Spring 1977): 167.

11 This is suggested by Joyce G. Baldwin, *Esther: An Introduction and Commentary*, Tyndale Old Testament Commentary 12 (Downers Grove, IL: InterVarsity Press, 1984), 108.

# BIBLIOGRAPHY

*Commentaries*

Baldwin, Joyce G. *Esther.* Tyndale Old Testament Commentary 12. Downers Grove, IL: InterVarsity Press, 1984.

Bardtke, Hans. *Das Buch Esther.* Kommentar zum Alten Testament 17/5. Gütersloh: Mohn, 1963.

Bechtel, Carol M. *Esther.* Interpretation. Louisville: John Knox, 2002.

Berlin, Adele. *Esther.* Philadelphia: Jewish Publication Society, 2001.

Bush, Frederic. *Ruth/Esther.* Word Biblical Commentary 9. Waco: Thomas Nelson, 1996.

Clines, David J. A. *Ezra, Nehemiah, Esther.* New Century Bible Commentary. Grand Rapids: Eerdmans, 1984.

Day, Linda M. *Esther.* Abingdon Old Testament Commentary. Nashville: Abingdon, 2005.

Dommershausen, Werner. *Ester.* Würzburg: Echter, 1980.

Duguid, Iain M. *Esther and Ruth.* Reformed Expository Commentary. Phillipsburg, NJ: P&R Publishing, 2005.

Fox, Michael V. *Character and Ideology in the Book of Esther.* 2nd ed. Grand Rapids: Eerdmans, 2001.

Gordis, Robert. *Megillat Esther: The Masoretic Hebrew Text, with Introduction, New Translation, and Commentary.* New York: Ktav, 1974.

Jobes, Karen H. *Esther.* The NIV Application Commentary. Grand Rapids: Zondervan, 1999.

Laniak, Timothy S. "Esther." Pages 167–274 in Leslie C. Allen and Timothy S. Laniak, *Ezra, Nehemiah, Esther.* New International Biblical Commentary. Peabody, MA: Hendrickson, 2003.

Levenson, Jon D. *Esther.* Old Testament Library. Louisville: Westminster John Knox, 1997.

McConville, J. G. *Ezra, Nehemiah, and Esther.* Daily Study Bible. Louisville: Westminster John Knox, 1985.

Moore, Carey A. *Esther: A New Translation with Introduction and Commentary.* Anchor Bible 7. Garden City, NY: Doubleday, 1982.

Paton, Lewis B. *A Critical and Exegetical Commentary on the Book of Esther.* The International Critical Commentary. New York: C. Scribner's Sons, 1908.

Wells, Samuel. "Esther." Pages 5–91 in Samuel Wells and George Sumner, *Esther and Daniel.* Brazos Theological Commentary on the Bible. Grand Rapids: Brazos Press, 2013.

*Other Works*

Albright, William F. "The Lachish Cosmetic Burner and Esther 2:12." Pages 25–32 in *A Light unto My Path: Old Testament Studies in Honor of Jacob M. Myers*. Edited by H. N. Bream, R. D. Hein, and C. A. Moore. Philadelphia: Temple University Press, 1974.

Allen, Lindsey. *The Persian Empire.* Chicago: University of Chicago Press, 2005.

Anderson, Gary A. *A Time to Mourn, a Time to Dance: The Expression of Grief and Joy in Israelite Religion.* University Park, PA: Pennsylvania State University Press, 1991.

Augustine. "On the Holy Trinity." In *Nicene and Post-Nicene Fathers: First Series.* Vol. 3. Edited by Philip Schaff. Peabody: Hendrickson, 2004.

———. "Sermon 263." In *Sermons: VII (230–272B).* Translated by Edmund Hill. The Works of Saint Augustine, Part 3-7. Hyde Park, NY: New City Press, 1993.

Bach, Alice. *Women, Seduction, and Betrayal in Biblical Narrative.* New York: Cambridge University Press, 1997.

Bar-Efrat, Shimon. *Narrative Art in the Bible.* 2nd ed. Journal for the Study of the Old Testament Supplement Series 70. Sheffield: Sheffield Academic Press, 1984.

Barth, Karl. *Church Dogmatics II.1: The Doctrine of God*. Edited by G. W. Bromiley and T. F. Torrance. Edinburgh: T. & T. Clark, 1957.

Beal, Timothy K. *The Book of Hiding: Gender, Ethnicity, Annihilation, and Esther.* London: Routledge, 1997.

Berg, Sandra Beth. *The Book of Esther: Motifs, Themes, and Structure.* Society of Biblical Literature Dissertation Series 44, Missoula, MT: Scholars Press, 1979.

Berkouwer, G. C. *The Providence of God.* Grand Rapids: Eerdmans, 1952.

Berlin, Adele. "The Book of Esther and Ancient Storytelling." *Journal of Biblical Literature* 120, no. 1 (Spring 2001): 3–14.

Bethge, Eberhard. "One of the Silent Bystanders? Dietrich Bonhoeffer on November 9, 1938." Pages 58-71 in *Friendship and Resistance: Essays on Dietrich Bonhoeffer.* Grand Rapids: Eerdmans, 1995.

Bickerman, Elias. *Four Strange Books of the Bible.* New York: Schocken, 1985.

Bloch, Abraham P. *The Biblical and Historical Background of Jewish Customs and Ceremonies.* New York: Ktav, 1980.

———. *The Biblical and Historical Background of the Jewish Holy Days.* New York: Ktav, 1978.

Brettler, Marc Zvi. *How to Read the Bible.* Philadelphia: Jewish Publication Society, 2005.

Briant, Pierre. *From Cyrus to Alexander: A History of the Persian Empire.* Translated by Peter T. Daniels. Winona Lake, IN: Eisenbrauns, 2002.

Brighton, Louis A. "The Book of Esther: Textual and Canonical Considerations." *Concordia Journal* 13, no. 3 (July 1987): 200–218.

Bronner, Leila L. "Reclaiming Esther: From Sex Object to Sage." *Jewish Bible Quarterly* 26, no. 1 (January–March 1998): 3–11.

Brooks, Thomas. "A Heavenly Cordial." Pages 410–34 in *The Complete Works of Thomas Brooks*. Vol. 6. Edinburgh: James Nichol, 1867.

Broyde, Michael J. "Defilement of the Hands, Canonization of the Bible, and the Special Status of Esther, Ecclesiastes, and Song of Songs." *Judaism* 44 (1995): 65–79.

Buechner, Frederick. *Now and Then: A Memoir of Vocation.* New York: HarperOne, 1983.

Burdell, George P. "Hiddenness and Revelation: Theology and Typology." *Atlanta Theological Review*, no. 4 (1999): 126–42.

Calvin, John. "Isaiah 13:3." *Commentary on the Book of the Prophet Isaiah.* Vol. 1. Translated by William Pringle. Grand Rapids: Christian Classics Ethereal Library. Available online at http://www.ccel.org/ccel/calvin/calcom13.xx.i.html.

Charnock, Stephen. "A Discourse of Divine Providence." In *The Complete Works of Stephen Charnock.* Vol. 1. Edinburgh: James Nichol, 1864.

Childs, Brevard S. *Introduction to the Old Testament as Scripture.* Philadelphia: Fortress, 1979.

Chrysostom, John. "Treatise to Prove that No One Can Harm the Man Who Does Not Injure Himself." In *Nicene and Post-Nicene Fathers: First Series.* Vol. 9. Edited by Philip Schaff. New York: Cosimo, 2007.

Clines, David J. A. *The Esther Scroll: The Story of the Story.* Journal for the Study of the Old Testament Supplement Series 30. Sheffield: JSOT Press, 1984.

Cohen, Jeffrey M. "Vashti—An Unsung Heroine." *Jewish Bible Quarterly* 24, no. 2 (April–June 1996): 103–6.

Collins, N. L. "Did Esther Fast on the 15th Nisan? An Extended Comment on Esther 3:12." *Revue Biblique* 100 (1993): 533–61.

Craig, Kenneth M., Jr., *Reading Esther: A Case for the Literary Carnivalesque.* Louisville: Westminster John Knox, 1995.

Crump, David. *Knocking on Heaven's Door: A New Testament Theology of Petitionary Prayer.* Grand Rapids: Baker Academic, 2006.

Cullman, Oscar. *Salvation in History.* Translated by S. G. Sowers. London: SCM, 1967.

Day, Linda. *Three Faces of a Queen: Characterization in the Books of Esther.* Journal for the Study of the Old Testament Supplement Series 186. Sheffield: Sheffield Academic Press, 1995.

Dehqani-Tafti, Hassan. *Design of My World: Pilgrimage to Christianity.* New York: Seabury Press, 1982.

———. *The Hard Awakening.* New York: Seabury Press, 1981.

De Troyer, Kristen. *The End of the Alpha Text of Esther: Translation and Narrative Technique in MT 8:1-17, LXX 8:1-17, and AT 7:14-41.* Society of Biblical Literature Septuagint and Cognate Studies Series 48. Atlanta: Society of Biblical Literature, 2000.

Dommershausen, Werner. *Die Estherrolle: Stil und Zeil einer alttestamentliches Schrift.* Stuttgarter Biblische Monographien 6. Stuttgart: Verlag Katholisches Bibelwerk, 1968.

Dorothy, Charles V. *The Books of Esther: Structure, Genre, and Textual Integrity.* Journal for the Study of the Old Testament Supplement Series 187. Sheffield: Sheffield Academic Press, 1997.

Duguid, Iain. "But Did They Live Happily Ever After? The Eschatology of the Book of Esther." *Westminster Theological Journal* 68 (2006): 85–98.

Flavel, John. *Divine Conduct; or, The Mystery of Providence.* London: Religious Tract Society, 1847.

Fleishman, Joseph. "Why Did Ahasuerus Consent to Annihilate the Jews?" *Journal of Northwest Semitic Languages* 25, no. 2 (1999): 41–58.

Foxe, John. *The New Foxe's Book of Martyrs.* North Brunswick: NJ: Bridge-Logos, 1997.

Fox, Michael V. "Three Esthers." Pages 50–60 in *The Book of Esther in Modern Research.* Edited by Leonard Greenspoon and Sidnie White Crawford. Journal for the Study of the Old Testament Supplement Series 380. London: T&T Clark, 2003.

Freedman, Amelia Devin. *God as an Absent Character in Biblical Hebrew Narrative: A Literary-Theoretical Study.* Studies in Biblical Literature 82. New York: Peter Lang, 2005.

Fried, Lisbeth S. "Towards the Ur-Text of Esther." *Journal for the Study of the Old Testament* 25, no. 88 (June 2000): 49–57.

Friedman, Richard Elliot. *The Disappearance of God: A Divine Mystery.* Boston: Little, Brown and Company, 1995.

Gan, Moshe. "The Book of Esther in Light of the Story of Joseph in Egypt." *Tarbiz* 31 (1961–62): 144–49.

Gerrish, B. A. "'To the Unknown God': Luther and Calvin on the Hiddenness of God." *The Journal of Religion* 53, no. 3 (July 1973): 263–92.

Gevaryahu, Haim M. I. "Esther Is a Story of Jewish Defense, not a Story of Jewish Revenge." *Jewish Bible Quarterly* 21, no. 1 (January 1993): 3–12.

Goldman, Stan. "Narrative and Ethical Ironies in Esther." *Journal for the Study of the Old Testament* 15, no. 47 (June 1990): 15–31.

Goodman, Philip. *The Purim Anthology.* Philadelphia: Jewish Publication Society, 1964.

———. "Religion, Wisdom and History in the Book of Esther—A New Solution to an Ancient Crux." *Journal of Biblical Literature* 100, no. 3 (September 1981): 359–88.

———. "Studies in the Esther Narrative." *Journal of Biblical Literature* 95, no. 1 (March 1976): 43–58.

Goswell, Gregory R. "Keeping God Out of the Book of Esther." *Evangelical Quarterly* 82, no. 2 (April 2010): 99–110.

Greenstein, Edward L. "A Jewish Reading of Esther." Pages 225–43 in *Judaic Perspectives on Ancient Israel.* Edited by Jacob Neusner, Baruch A. Levine, and Ernest S. Frerichs. Philadelphia: Fortress, 1987.

Gregory, Bradley C. "Megillot and Festivals." Pages 457–64 in *Dictionary of the Old Testament: Wisdom, Poetry & Writings.* Edited by Tremper Longman III and Peter Enns. Downers Grove, IL: IVP Academic, 2008.

———. "Purim." Pages 631–34 in *Dictionary of the Old Testament: Wisdom, Poetry & Writings.* Edited by Tremper Longman III and Peter Enns. Downers Grove, IL: IVP Academic, 2008.

Grossman, Jonathan. *Esther: The Outer Narrative and the Hidden Reading.* Siphrut 6. Winona Lake, IN: Eisenbrauns, 2001.

Groves, Elizabeth. "Double Take: Another Look at the Second Gathering of Virgins of Esther 2.19a." Pages 91-110 in *The Book of Esther in Modern Research*. Journal for the Study of the Old Testament Supplement Series 380. Edited by Leonard Greenspoon and Sidnie White Crawford. London: T&T Clark, 2003.

Hallo, William W. "The First Purim." *Biblical Archaeologist* 46, no. 1 (Winter 1983): 19–26.

Harris, Monford. "Purim, Celebration of Disorder." *Judaism* 26, no. 2 (Spring 1977): 161–70.

Heltzer, Michael. "The Book of Esther: Where Does Fiction Start and History End?" *Bible Review* 8, no. 1 (February 1992): 25–30, 41.

Henry, Matthew. *Commentary on the Whole Bible, Volume II: Joshua to Esther*. Grand Rapids: Christian Classics Ethereal Library, 2009.

Holt, Mack P. *The French Wars of Religion, 1562–1629*. Cambridge: Cambridge University Press, 1995.

Horn, Siegfried H. "Mordecai, A Historical Problem." *Biblical Research* 9 (1964): 14–25.

Howard-Snyder, Daniel, and Paul K. Moser. "Introduction: The Hiddenness of God." Pages 1–23 in *Divine Hiddenness*. Edited by Daniel Howard-Snyder and Paul K. Moser. New York: Cambridge University Press, 2002.

Humpreys, W. Lee. "The Story of Esther and Mordecai: An Early Jewish Novella." Pages 97-113 in *Saga, Legend, Tale, Novella, Fable: Narrative Forms in Old Testament Literature*. Edited by George W. Coats. Journal for the Study of the Old Testament Supplement Series 35. Sheffield: JSOT Press, 1985.

Hyman, Ronald T. "Esther 3:3: The Question with No Response." *Jewish Bible Quarterly* 22, no. 2 (April–June 1994): 103–9.

Jackowski, Karol. "Holy Disobedience in Esther." *Theology Today* 45, no. 4 (January 1989): 403–14.

Jacobs, Jonathan. "Characterizing Esther from the Outset: The Contribution of the Story in Esther 2:1-20." *Journal of Hebrew Scriptures* 8 (2008): 2–13.

Jobes, Karen H. *The Alpha-Text of Esther: Its Character and Relationship to the Masoretic Text*. Society of Biblical Literature Dissertation Series 153. Atlanta: Scholars Press, 1996.

Jones, Bruce William. "Two Misconceptions about the Book of Esther." *Catholic Biblical Quarterly* 39, no. 2 (April 1977): 171–81.

Katz, Ben Zion. "Irrevocability of Persian Law in the Scroll of Esther." *Jewish Bible Quarterly* 31, no. 2 (April–June 2003): 94–96.

LaCocque, André. *The Feminine Unconventional: Four Subversive Figures in Israel's Tradition*. Overtures to Biblical Theology. Minneapolis: Fortress, 1990.

———. "Haman in the Book of Esther." *Hebrew Annual Review* 11 (1987): 207–22.

———. *Shame and Honor in the Book of Esther.* Society of Biblical Literature Dissertation Series 165. Atlanta: Scholars Press, 1998.

Lewis, Alan E. *Between Cross and Resurrection: A Theology of Holy Saturday.* Grand Rapids: Eerdmans, 2001.

MacDonald, Gordon. "The Mark of the Artist." Sermon, October 16, 1994. Text available online at http://www.csec.org/index.php/archives/23-member-archives/597-gordon-macdonald-program-3803.

Marshall, Paul, Lela Gilbert, and Nina Shea. *Persecuted: The Global Assault on Christians.* Nashville: Thomas Nelson, 2013.

McGrath, Alister. *Luther's Theology of the Cross: Martin Luther's Theological Breakthrough.* Oxford: Blackwell, 1985.

Metaxas, Eric. *Amazing Grace: William Wilberforce and the Heroic Campaign to End Slavery.* New York: HarperCollins, 2007.

Miller, Patrick D. "For Such a Time as This." *Princeton Seminary Bulletin*, n.s., 27, no. 2 (2006): 146–55.

Oppenheim, A. Leo. "On Royal Gardens in Mesopotamia." *Journal of Near Eastern Studies* 24, no. 4 (October 1965): 328–33.

Origen. *Homilies on Numbers.* Downers Grove: IVP Academic, 2009.

Owen, John. "The Death of Death in the Death of Christ." Pages 157–421 in *The Works of John Owen*. Vol. 10. Carlisle, PA: Banner of Truth, 1978.

Pascal, Blaise. *Pensées*. Translated by A. J. Krailsheimer. New York: Penguin, 1995.

Peterson, Eugene. *Five Smooth Stones for Pastoral Work*. Grand Rapids: Eerdmans, 1980.

Radday, Yehuda. "Esther with Humour." Pages 295–313 in *On Humour and the Comic in the Hebrew Bible*. Edited by Yehuda T. Radday and Athalya Brenner. Journal for the Study of the Old Testament Supplement Series 92. Sheffield: Almond Press, 1990.

Rosenthal, Ludwig A. "Die Josephsgeschichte mit den Buchern Ester und Daniel verglichen." *Zeitschrift für die alttestamentliche Wissenschaft* 15, no. 1 (January 1895): 278–84.

Rossow, Francis C. "Literary Artistry in the Book of Esther and Its Theological Significance." *Concordia Journal* 13, no. 3 (July 1987): 219–33.

Rudofsky, Bernard. *The Unfashionable Human Body*. Garden City, NY: Doubleday, 1971.

Ryken, Leland. *Words of Delight: A Literary Introduction to the Bible*. 2nd ed. Grand Rapids: Baker, 1993.

Ryle, J. C. *Expository Thoughts on the Gospels: St. Luke*. Vol. 2. New York: Robert Carter and Brothers, 1879.

Sasson, Jack. "Esther." Pages 335–42 in *The Literary Guide to the Bible*. Edited by Robert Alter and Frank Kermode. Cambridge, MA: Belknap, 1987.

Shakespeare, William. *Hamlet*. In *The Complete Works of William Shakespeare*. Vol. 2. Garden City: NY, Nelson Doubleday, 1979.

Shanks, Hershel, et al. "Losing Faith: Who Did and Who Didn't." *Biblical Archaeology Review* 33, no. 2 (March–April 2007): 50-57.

Shea, William H. "Esther and History." *Concordia Journal* 13, no. 3 (July 1987): 234–48.

Sproul, R. C. *The Invisible Hand*. Dallas: Word, 1997.

Spurgeon, Charles Haddon. "God's Providence." Sermon, New Park Street Chapel, Southwark, London, October 15, 1908. Available online at http://www.spurgeon.org/sermons/3114.htm.

Sternberg, Meir. *The Poetics of Biblical Narrative: Ideological Literature and the Drama of Reading.* Bloomington: Indiana University Press, 1987.

Terrien, Samuel. *The Elusive Presence: Toward a New Biblical Theology.* Eugene, OR: Wipf and Stock, 2000.

Thornton, Timothy C. G. "The Crucifixion of Haman and the Scandal of the Cross" *Journal of Theological Studies*, n.s., 37, no. 2 (1986): 419–26.

Tkacz, Catherine Brown. "Esther as a Type of Christ and the Jewish Celebration of Purim." *Studia Patristica* 44 (2010): 183–87.

van Inwagen, Peter. "What Is the Problem of the Hiddenness of God?" Pages 24–32 in *Divine Hiddenness.* Edited by Daniel Howard-Snyder and Paul K. Moser. New York: Cambridge University Press, 2002.

Walfish, Barry Dov. "Kosher Adultery? The Mordecai-Esther-Ahasuerus Triangle in Midrash and Exegesis." *Prooftexts* 22, no. 3 (Fall 2002): 305–33.

Walsh, Carey Ellen. "Under the Influence: Trust and Risk in Biblical Family Drinking." *Journal for the Study of the Old Testament* 25, no. 90 (September 2000): 13–29.

Warfield, B. B. *Biblical Doctrines.* Carlisle: Banner of Truth, 1988.

Watson, Thomas. *A Body of Divinity.* Carlisle, PA: Banner of Truth, 1957.

Webb, Barry G. *Five Festal Garments: Christian Reflections on the Song of Songs, Ruth, Lamentations, Ecclesiastes, and Esther.* New Studies in Biblical Theology. Downers Grove, IL: IVP Academic, 2000.

———. "Reading Esther as Holy Scripture." *Reformed Theological Review* 52, no. 1 (January–April 1993): 23–35.

Wechsler, Michael G. "Shadow and Fulfillment in the Book of Esther." *Bibliotheca Sacra* 154, no. 615 (July–September 1997): 275–84.

Weiland, Forrest S. "Historicity, Genre, and Narrative Design in the Book of Esther." *Bibliotheca Sacra* 159, no. 634 (April–June 2002): 151–65.

———. "Literary Clues to God's Providence in the Book of Esther." *Bibliotheca Sacra* 160, no. 637 (January 2003): 34–47.

Welch, Edward. *Addictions: A Banquet in the Grave, Finding Hope in the Power of the Gospel.* Phillipsburg: P&R Publishing, 2001.

Wetter, Anne-Mareike. "How Jewish Is Esther? Or: How Is Esther Jewish? Tracing Ethnic and Religious Identity in a Diaspora Narrative," *Zeitschrift für die alttestamentliche Wissenschaft* 123, no. 4 (December 2011): 596–603.

Wiebe, John M. "Esther 4:14: 'Will Relief and Deliverance Arise for the Jews from Another Place?' " *Catholic Biblical Quarterly* 53, no. 3 (July 1991): 409–15.

Wiesel, Elie. *Night.* Translated by Stella Rodway. New York: Bantam Books, 1987.

Wright, N. T. *Evil and the Justice of God.* Downers Grove: InterVarsity, 2006.

———. *Paul: A Fresh Perspective.* Minneapolis: Fortress, 2009.

Yamauchi, Edwin. "Archaeological Backgrounds of the Exilic and Postexilic Era, Part 2: The Archaeological Background of Esther." *Bibliotheca Sacra* 137, no. 546 (April–June 1980): 99–117.

———. "Mordecai, the Persepolis Tablets, and the Susa Escavations." *Vetus Testamentum* 42, no. 2 (April 1992): 272–75.

———. *Persia and the Bible.* Grand Rapids: Baker, 1990.

# INDEX OF SCRIPTURE